PENGUIN BOOKS

Another Bad Day at the Office?

Jeremy Bullmore was born in 1929. His first job, in 1954, was as a trainee copywriter with J. Walter Thompson in London and he stayed with that agency until his retirement in 1987. He became successively copywriter, writer/producer, creative group head and head of television; then from 1964 to 1975 head of the creative department, and from 1976 to 1987 chairman, London. From 1981 to 1987 he was chairman of the Advertising Association. Since 1988 Jeremy Bullmore has been a non-executive director of the Guardian Media Group plc and WPP Group plc and is the immediate past President of NABS.

As well as numerous radio and television appearances, he has written prolifically and lectured in many countries on marketing and advertising. He is a weekly columnist for *Campaign* and writes regularly for *Management Today* and *Market Leader*. He has received both the London Publicity Club's Cup and the Design and Art Directors' Association President's Award for outstanding contributions to advertising. He is a Fellow of the Institute of Practitioners in Advertising and was awarded a CBE in 1985.

Jeremy Bullmore is also the author of *Behind the Scenes in Advertising* (NTC Publications, new edition, 1998).

Another Bad Day at the Office?

Essential Advice on Workaday Problems

Jeremy Bullmore

PENGUIN BOOKS

PENGUIN BOOKS
Published by the Penguin Group

Penguin Books Ltd, 80 Strand, London WC2R 0RL, England
Penguin Putnam Inc., 375 Hudson Street, New York, New York 10014, USA
Penguin Books Australia Ltd, 250 Camberwell Road, Camberwell, Victoria 3124, Australia
Penguin Books Canada Ltd, 10 Alcorn Avenue, Toronto, Ontario, Canada M4V 3B2
Penguin Books India (P) Ltd, 11, Community Centre, Panchsheel Park, New Delhi – 110 017, India
Penguin Books (NZ) Ltd, Cnr Rosedale and Airborne Roads, Albany, Auckland, New Zealand
Penguin Books (South Africa) (Pty) Ltd, 24 Sturdee Avenue, Rosebank 2196, South Africa

Penguin Books Ltd, Registered Offices: 80 Strand, London WC2R 0RL, England

On the World Wide Web at www.penguin.com

First published 2001
3

Copyright © Jeremy Bullmore, 2001
All rights reserved

The moral right of the author has been asserted

Set in Minion and Officina
Typeset by Rowland Phototypesetting Ltd, Bury St Edmunds, Suffolk
Printed in England by Clays Ltd, St Ives plc

For PB

Contents

Acknowledgements

It was Rufus Olins, of *Management Today*, who first suggested a monthly problem column; and then some years later, a book. I'm doubly grateful to him. My thanks are also due to Francesca Cunningham and Rebecca Hoar, also of *Management Today*, who have kept the problems coming; and to Stuart Proffitt, of Penguin, for giving it all some sense and shape.

Preface

The word work must be one of the most hard-working words in the English language.

There are those whose only ambition in life is to give up work completely, so much do they hate it; and there are those who say, and mean, 'I live for my work.' It's odd that we should have only one word to convey two such incompatible extremes.

This book is for those for whom work is somewhere in between: for people who, yes, do have to work, but who are lucky enough to have jobs which they mainly enjoy; who, given the choice, would probably go on working rather than stop altogether; yet who find parts of their working life frustrating, overdemanding, unrewarding or all three.

Their single biggest problem is not the nature of their work but the nature of human nature. Most work problems are people problems.

The comic strip occasion has its roots in life. Man or woman home from work, bag or briefcase hurled on to floor. 'Another bad day at the office, dear?' And out pours a stream of bottled-up bile and bewilderment. About the boss; about the client; about the IT idiot who made the whole system crash; about the new graduate trainee; about the best friend; about Norman and about Wendy.

This book is also for bosses: who are also people, and often with bosses of their own. Bosses are constantly confounded by the contrariness of their staff; by their unreasonable demands and perpetual dissatisfactions. And because so few bosses are formally trained for the job, they fret quite a lot about how to be a good one.

It isn't easy. If you believed some of the more confident management books, you could be forgiven for thinking that running a company, getting the best out of people, being competitively successful, was simply a matter of following a few simple rules. Establish goals, communicate them throughout, set standards, raise the bar, evaluate, reward. And so on.

All admirable actions, certainly; but the books forget that people at work are still people: just as quirky, just as vulnerable to grief, just as likely to feel lust or disgust, just as changeable as they are when at home or on holiday.

As any piece of research confirms, it's the company of other people that tops the list of what makes going off to work attractive. Yet it's those very same people – other people, of course – who then start ruining it all.

The comic strip occasion is true in another respect. Few of us, however baffled and frustrated we may feel, try to sort things out in the office; or even let our feelings show. We save them up for our luckless partners.

Bosses find it hard to admit doubt and indecision to colleagues:

it seems to concede inadequacy and jeopardize respect. And underlings are just as hesitant – perhaps because admitting anxiety to a colleague is to expose one's vulnerability to someone who may also, in some ways, be a competitor.

Apart from home, the most popular place for the venting of workaday fury is the pub. I once heard an indignant thirty-year-old retailing at enormous length the injustices to which he was being routinely subjected. 'When things go well,' he said, his voice rising to new levels of self-pity, 'who takes the credit? He does, of course. But when things go badly, it's a different story, I can tell you. He's nowhere to be seen, you can be sure of that, and *I'm* the scopegate!' A wonderful word, scopegate – but it totally punctured his appeal for sympathy.

This reluctance to be open about workplace dissatisfactions actually in the workplace may in part explain the popularity and high readership enjoyed by agony columns. It's reassuring to know that you're not alone; that others out there have felt the same. And, just occasionally, the answers may even be helpful.

So I hope this book may both entertain and instruct. And if some of the answers suggest that the fault may lie not so much with our colleagues as with ourselves – well, that's how I think it often is.

1 | *How can I work with people like this around me?*

We spend a lot of time at work in close proximity to other people. And unfortunately, unlike ourselves, other people have deficiencies.

Some of these deficiences are work-related: erratic time-keeping; a marked reluctance to stay late and help out; an unnerving inaccuracy with figures. And some will be personal and petty: Sandra rakes her hair back with her fingers; William whistles through his teeth; Colin is a slimy schemer who sucks up to the boss and gets away with it.

Even when minor, other people's bad habits, witnessed day after day with silent distaste, can rapidly generate major dissatisfactions. You can always tell when this is happening to you; you find the phrase 'and another thing' constantly occurring to you.

And if we're honest with ourselves, there will be times when our irritation is prompted not by colleagues' personal habits but by their evident success.

There are no all-purpose solutions to problems such as these. A serious attempt to see things through the eyes of others usually helps. And more often than not, an early and open admission of your feelings *will prevent that minor irritation from developing into a festering wound.*

I find one of my board colleagues extremely irritating. I think his ideas may be good but his voice and manner put me off. Unfortunately, my chairman seems to get on well with him. How can I overcome my bias?

I strongly suspect that it's not his voice and his manner that piss you off: it's the fact that his ideas are good and that he gets on well with your chairman.

Now, please don't throw your crayons on the floor. Just ask yourself these questions – and answer them as dispassionately as you can.

Do you feel in competition with this colleague? Do you, at heart, think he's better than you at some things? Does your chairman think your colleague's ideas are better than your own?

If, however reluctantly, you say yes at least once, then you're not suffering from anything as trivial as bias: you've got good old-fashioned envy corroding away inside you. And once you've acknowledged the presence of that entirely human condition, you'll be well on your way to recovery.

First, list all the things you know you do well – and do better than he does. (If you can't think of anything, call your favourite headhunter immediately.)

Then, grab the first opportunity that comes up for you and him to work together on an important project. Do only those things you know you do well. Allow him to do those things he does better than you. Be heroically forbearing if he sometimes trespasses on to your territory. It will soon become clear to both of you (and to your chairman) that you have complementary skills.

If the project proves successful, resist the temptation to claim any credit. (But feel free to enjoy some small, private pleasure at what you've achieved.)

And when you're having a drink together to celebrate your shared triumph, you might even tease him a little about his voice and his manner. (Though by then, of course, you may not find them irritating.)

One of my fellow directors (and a friend) is articulate, professional and successful but always has to know the answer to everything and leaves me and others feeling irritated and somehow diminished. He never seems to be able to admit he might be ignorant or wrong about anything or subject to normal vulnerabilities. As a result, I am finding it very difficult to maintain a proper relationship with him.

Are you sure this unattractive person is a friend? And if he is, are you sure you're being fair in your description of him?

You tell me that he's 'articulate, professional and successful' and leaves you and others 'feeling diminished'. My first and unworthy suspicion is that he leaves you feeling diminished simply because he's better at some things than you are and quite a lot more successful.

'No, no, no!' I hear you cry. 'It's not like that at all! He's a smug and self-important shit!' So OK, cool down now. I accept your verdict – but only on condition that you stop pretending (to me and to yourself) that he's your friend. You know perfectly well that you do not like this person – but are reluctant to say so out loud in case it smacks of envy and sour grapes.

There – you've said it. You should be feeling better already.

Abandoning any pretence at friendship frees you up in two ways. First, you can redefine what you call a 'proper relationship'. You don't have to go on being matey through gritted teeth. No more dutiful drinks after work or shared family photographs. You can just be as civil as you need to be in order to work together. And secondly, you can now mock him lightly from time to time about his relentless omniscience. If he finds that an unfriendly act, that's fine. He's no friend of yours, re-member?

And if the mocking works, and he mends his ways, and becomes an altogether more likeable person . . . who knows? You might even find a friend – but a real one, this time.

I take regular cigarette breaks during the day, but I get all my work done. Last week, three of my colleagues took me aside to say they found it unacceptable that I should take so much time out of the day for cigarette breaks, and asked me to cut down. I don't see why I should so long as I'm doing my job well. But there's now a nasty atmosphere, and I'm wondering whether I should do as they say.

I'm willing to bet that none of the three colleagues who took you aside so officiously is also a smoker. It's quite extraordinary (and rather scary) how the image of smoking has changed over the last forty years or so. In the first of the books, *Casino Royale*, published in the early fifties, Ian Fleming established James Bond's heroic characteristics by having him light 'his seventieth cigarette of the day'. Now you see smokers huddled in doorways, socially acceptable only to each other.

As I'm sure you suspect yourself, your colleagues aren't really concerned about the number of breaks you take; they're exuding moral disapproval of you because you smoke. They see you as part of the addicted classes; while they, smug buggers all of them, are not.

So my sympathies are with you; but, I fear, unless you want to make a job move, it is you who needs to be seen to change. So cut down on the breaks – and do it without truculence or ostentation.

I know it's not fair, but you must. Making concessions when principle suggests you needn't is often a sign of maturity rather than feebleness. You're even allowed to take some secret pleasure from it.

A last thought occurs to me. The fact that all three took you aside suggests that there's an unhealthy gang atmosphere in your workplace, from which you are excluded. If that's the case, a move may be necessary anyway.

I job-share with another colleague, but I keep finding that he has undone the work I have done. He also misplaces files and contact details, forgets to pass on messages, and neglects to

tell me which areas need following up on my days in the office.
I have tried to gently mention it to him once or twice, with no
result. I'm thinking of taking the problem to someone more
senior, but this is a trial job-share scheme which I requested
and I really don't want to jeopardize it.

This man's work habits are so comprehensively shambolic as to
seem actively planned. And I can't help wondering if they are.

Have you wondered, yourself, if this catalogue of incompetence might just be deliberate? You say that your job-sharing
arrangement is something of an experiment; so certainly one
explanation for his behaviour (and one that would also cover
his reluctance to improve) would be a determination on his part
to see the experiment fail. You can test this possibility by noting
whether his inefficiencies seem to be disproportionately lavished
on you or whether he distributes them indiscriminately.

If he's as unreliable with others as he is with you – in other
words, if he's clearly one of the world's natural no-hopers – you
needn't worry too much about taking your misgivings to a
superior: his heroic inadequacies will certainly have been noted
and a nudge from you may be all that is needed.

It gets more difficult if he's been busy making life extremely
difficult for you while performing for others with charm and
competence.

I can only suggest, if you haven't already done it, that you
start making a list of his errors and omissions. However distasteful you find it, sooner or later you're going to have to bring
things to a head – and you'll need to have a strong and sober
case.

Please don't be petty, though, or you'll lose all credibility. Confine yourself to clear, demonstrable examples of negligence – and hope that justice prevails.

I have a middle-management colleague for whom I have no professional respect. Like me, she is in her early thirties, but spends most of her time flirting with male colleagues and gossiping rather than supporting her own staff and getting reports done on time. Her reluctance to do what she has been employed to do backfires on me as her staff come to me for guidance and I have to compensate for the work she isn't doing. The obvious solution is to discuss this with my boss but he is a close friend of hers. I find it very frustrating that someone can get away with doing so little in such a key job.

First, search your own mind thoroughly for evidence of envy. All clear? None there? Quite sure? OK – fine.

Now take her out to lunch. And with absolutely no heat and no tedious repetitions, tell her exactly what you've told me. Show her your letter, why not? Above all, avoid the phrase '. . . and another thing'. Pour another glass of wine. Even if not much improvement occurs, you won't have done anything you might later regret.

Six months ago, I started a new job as head of an online news service. I believe I'm doing a good job, but I've found out from a member of my team that my middle manager has been trying to turn my staff against me when they go out for their weekly 'boys' night outs' and also that he's told the company director I am lazy and inadequate. I'm very shocked, and want to take action without being branded an 'hysterical woman'. What's the best course of action?

This sounds nasty. There are far too many people talking behind other people's backs. What good does this team member think he's doing by telling you what your middle manager is saying about you? And does he stay silent while all this is going on, in tacit agreement – or does he stand up for you? It sounds to me like one of those all-too-familiar instances of contagious bitchiness that can break out in any organization. It's surprising how perfectly agreeable people can start stirring things up when the example is set by someone senior.

From what you say, it's your middle manager who's spreading the infection. If you can only neutralize him, you can stop the disease in its tracks.

Don't worry too much about the hysterical woman bit: there's almost certainly a bit of old-fashioned sexism going on here but you shouldn't make an issue of it. Go and see your company director. You've been doing the job for six months now: can you please have a no-holds-barred appraisal – in writing? If the appraisal is good, ask him if he thinks your team is happy. Better not mention your team member's gossip – it might be just that. If again he gives you the thumbs up, say that there's been a bit of initial uncertainty in your team and that you'd find it very helpful if he'd do a short note or e-mail, marking your first half year in the job and confirming your leadership.

That should do the trick – but only, of course, if your appraisal really is positive. If it isn't, then you've got another problem altogether.

When it gets personal . . .

Managers who behave as if personal problems are what people encounter exclusively at home will be either deeply disappointed or rank bad managers. In any company in which the quality of the people counts – and that should mean every company – there will be problems of immense delicacy to solve: ranging from the seemingly trivial to the deeply moving. And it's no good shrugging them off on the grounds that, at work, only business considerations count. Like it or not, personal problems and business considerations can never be neatly divorced.

Things can get tricky when personal feelings start affecting professional judgement. Others observe that Clive is beginning to favour Clare and soon there's a general sense of injustice abroad.

The more serious personal problems are often acutely embarrassing. They demand huge applications of tiptoeing tact – and, above all, time.

Most of those in trouble crave a sympathetic hearing. As a boss, you may believe (and will certainly hope) that a single conversation is all that's needed – but it won't be. However short of it you are, generosity with your time will usually give far greater comfort than the most carefully chosen words of sympathy.

Much unhappiness, and occasional misery, often lurk in the workplace; and mainly because both bosses and bossed seem to think that to acknowledge it is somehow unseemly.

My MD is making me feel uncomfortable. I am a female account manager at a PR firm. He asked me to go with him to a client meeting. The client's offices are close, so we set out on foot, but the meeting was a ruse. Instead, he stopped at a shirt shop and asked me to pick out for him the shirts I liked. I refused and now there is an atmosphere between us. Did I do the right thing?

You may have done the right thing; but, by the sound of it, you didn't do it in the right way.

You made the instant assumption that your MD's motives were far from professional – and I'm sure you're right. (It sounds as if he's already attached and you don't seem to like him much anyway.)

His ruse, of course, was designed to test your reaction – without leaving himself open to outright rejection. In his dreams, no doubt, you accepted his suggestion with delight, held up a shirt to see if it matched his eyes and then suggested that he might like to buy one for you as well because you always wore men's shirts in bed. That would have made him a very happy managing director indeed.

Instead, you cut him off at the knees, making an open assumption about his motives and no attempt whatever to preserve his self-esteem. Hence the atmosphere.

The fact that he deserved every bit of it is neither here nor there: it's the working relationship you're concerned about.

What could you have done? It's never easy to think of nifty wheezes on the spur of the moment, but it might have got interesting if you'd said, 'Oh, I'm hopeless on men's shirts but Derek's terrific. He's picking me up this evening – so why don't we all three come back then?'

Come to think of it, bringing Derek into the conversation from now on (even if he doesn't exist) might encourage your predatory boss to go hunting elsewhere.

Suddenly I am having to play office politics. My manager's boss has taken me into his confidence and criticized my manager who he seems to want out of the company. I like the company and am keen to progress. But I don't know how candid I can be with either of them.

I smell rats – and Rat Number One is your manager's boss. He shouldn't be discussing your manager with you at all – let alone critically. It puts you in a totally impossible position.

But I also smell something more than simply office politics. As you describe it, your manager's boss's behaviour is not just rat-like but puzzling. As the senior person, he should be able to get your manager out of the company easily enough if he thinks it's necessary. And how does he think confiding in you is going to help him, anyway?

So it occurs to me to ask: are your manager and your manager's boss by any chance men? And are you, by any chance, not?

If I'm right in this guess, then at least it begins to sort out some motives. Rat Number One hopes that you'll be impressed by his seniority and flattered by his confidences. Discussing your manager gives him an excuse to talk to you. And once you've started sharing a few little secrets, thinks Rat – who knows what further intimacies might follow?

My advice is to avoid at all costs being party to any further conversations about your manager – and make it clear why. If you're happy working for your manager, and rate him highly, then say so. You may be surprised to find how swiftly Rat starts changing his tune.

And whatever you do, resist the temptation to involve your manager in all this, even by innuendo. It will only make things even more complicated.

At fifty-two, I look around my company and realize that my colleagues just get younger and younger. I worry that my days may be numbered. Is there anything I can do? I am due a sabbatical later this year and have thought about going to California and getting myself a face-lift.

Oh, wow. What kind of business are you in, for goodness sake? I've no idea if you're male or female – but whichever you are, it's time you grew up.

It sounds as if you've been with the same company for some time. Is it just for your looks that they've kept you on? Or are you actually quite good at something? That's the only question you need to concentrate on.

This obsession with age and appearance is often the hallmark of people who are extremely self-centred. When you walk into a room, I bet you're wondering what people are thinking of you. The truth – painful perhaps to you, but wonderfully liberating – is that they almost certainly aren't thinking anything about you.

In the same way, I bet you're the only person in your company who's given a moment's thought to your age and looks.

However, if you're determined to be the centre of ridicule, you can do no better than come back from California looking like Zsa Zsa Gabor. Then you really might have something to worry about.

One of my colleagues has a bad hygiene problem. He looks clean but it's like he never washes. Some days he smells so bad people in our department baulk at having meetings with him, let alone sitting next to him. Should I tell him and, if so, how? What if it's something medical?

I'm not being facetious (please believe me) when I ask: does he have a best friend? If he does, that's where you should start. And don't just say, 'Does Frank know he stinks to high heaven?' – even best friends might find that a bit direct. Instead, raise the medical point you're right to be concerned about. Ask, with genuine concern, if Frank has a skin problem – and see what develops from that.

But from what you say, and from what you don't, I suspect he doesn't have a best friend – at least at work. Nor, I suspect, does he have a partner at home. The chances are that he smells as bad as he does because he lives alone, doesn't change his clothes very often, and thinks that anti-perspirants are strictly for airline stewards. You can have two showers a day and still smell horrible if you wear the same shirt all the time. (Or so I'm told.)

So there's nothing for it but a direct approach from you: and here you must be quite supernaturally delicate.

Choose a sandwich in the park, or a pub or wine bar: not the office. The crucial moment is obviously the opening. Get around to home life. How long has he lived alone? Does he do his own cooking, shopping? Does he use a laundrette? You'll learn enough from this not to blunder too badly if he really does have a medical condition.

Tell him that when you first left your parents' home, you used to wear the same shirt and socks for days on end. Wait for some response and adjust accordingly.

Only when it seems right should you say that there are times when he reminds you of your own early, living-alone days: quite nostalgic, really. You should be light about all this, and slightly amused – but the box is now open.

I expect you think this is an absurdly laborious way of going about it, and it may well be quite unnecessary. But remember: you can always progress from extreme subtlety to upfront confrontation, but never vice versa. And there's a person's self-esteem at stake.

My immediate boss has told me that if I want to progress in my City firm, I shouldn't wear the Armani suit I have just bought in the sales. It seems several partners object to its 'non-U' green/ brown colour. I have so far been something of a high-flier. Should I just take his advice or try to discuss it?

It would be quite easy to work yourself up into a quivering mass of indignation over this. How dare these ancient relics impose their ludicrously outdated standards on a young, thrusting high-flier such as yourself? It's good to see you're not reacting like that.

Most jobs, explicitly or implicitly, impose dress codes of some kind – and it's rarely a Humiliating Subjugation of True Self to go along with them. Anyway, they change – almost imperceptibly, I grant you, but they do.

I don't suppose you'd think of wearing shorts to work, for example (even Armani shorts), or even an open-necked shirt. Yet there are many professional firms these days where neither custom would raise an eyebrow.

I think you should take your boss's advice, which is presumably well meant, and just see how things develop. Sooner or later, greeny-brown Armani suits will be perfectly acceptable; then commonplace; and some time after that, derisively traditional.

And here's a confident forecast. I bet that by the time you're a senior partner yourself, you'll be expressing mild disapproval about some young high-flier's unfortunate predilection for nose-studs.

…no control over my blushing and am concerned
…promoted to chief economist at my company, it
…ok unprofessional, overemotional or an open book.
…d I do?

It would, I suppose, be facetious to suggest that a chief economist who reads like an open book should be deeply reassuring to his or her company. The trouble is, blushing may also suggest that the blusher has something to hide – which is presumably not so welcome.

So far, of course (as you will have been the first to notice), my answer has conformed to the sad convention about blushing. To the sufferer, it can be a deeply distracting affliction, sapping the confidence and the self-esteem; while to colleagues and friends, insensitive creatures all, it's just a bit of a laugh – an excuse for a tease. So forgive me.

If your blushing is causing you serious distress, you should start by seeking professional advice. Talk to your GP if you've got a sympathetic one, but don't exclude alternative treatment. I've heard of cases where hypnotherapy has helped, for example.

Worrying about worrying can be corrosive. You need to break the circle somehow. And the only other tack – which requires superhuman quantities of chutzpah – is to draw attention to your blushing whenever you feel a good one brewing up. Tell people you blush. Warn them to watch out for it. Say, 'Wow, that was a good one.' It's coming close to asking the impossible and you may find the very thought of it unbearable. But if you think you might just manage it, give it a go. Someone I know tried this trick – and was almost disappointed to discover that he never blushed again.

My boss seems to have singled me out for attention – which is great – but to such an extent that it's embarrassing. He sings my praises to all my colleagues, even when the credit isn't really mine and I've said so. I don't think he realizes, but it's starting to become divisive. Should I have a word with him?

He fancies you. It's not clear from your question whether you're a her or a him: but whichever, he fancies you. And I can't believe you needed me to tell you that.

Which in turn makes me think that you quite enjoy it all. There's something not wholly convincing about your protestations of embarrassment and disclaimers of credit. I can quite understand the discomfort of your colleagues: no wonder it's all becoming a bit divisive.

If you really want to put a stop to all this, then you must be ruthlessly self-disciplined. However 'great' you find it (your word), never look pleased when he singles you out. Don't lower the eyelashes and murmur little bashful things: that's exactly what spurs him on. Shrug, laugh, exchange raised eyebrows with the colleagues, move on. As soon as he stops fancying you he'll stop singling you out.

My competitor has started abusing me and my company in the local press and, I'm told, at local networking functions. I don't want to get heavy or start a 'war of words' but I worry that his inaccurate remarks may damage my business. Should I take action and, if so, what?

I expect you've already spoken to your lawyer. If not, you must. From what you say, a broadside on legal letterheading would seem amply justified; and, if couched in the fiercest prose your man can muster, it could be all you need to do. This may be what you mean by getting heavy but I can't see what you stand to lose.

That should certainly take care of the abuse in the local press. (Your lawyer may think that an open copy of his letter sent to the Editor would also be a canny wheeze.)

The tittle-tattle at local networking functions is harder to deal with. What, I wonder, is the nature of his tattle? What, exactly, is he accusing you of? You worry about starting 'a war of words' – and your worry worries me. I sense you think you might not come out of it too well.

If I'm right, then maybe your case isn't quite as watertight as you'd like it to be. Some of your competitor's slagging-off might even have a grain of truth to it.

So if it needs it, tidy up your act – and then recruit some friends: maybe those who've already told you what's going on at these networking functions. Ask them to note down any inaccurate and damaging comments made by your competitor and get them witnessed. Then, armed with these, go back to your lawyer.

Under no circumstances write long, aggrieved letters to your local newspaper. Letters pages are widely read so you'll simply multiply the number of people who know you've been accused of some vaguely dodgy behaviour.

However, you say that some of his accusations are 'inaccurate'. If they are demonstrably so, you should write the shortest of letters to that effect, check it with your lawyer and insist that it be printed for the record. Otherwise, your cuttings file will for ever find you guilty.

One of my colleagues has recently returned to work after the death of a very close family member, and I'm finding it hard to know how to treat them. They're not their normal self and I don't know whether it's best to mention the bereavement or not. What is the best way to behave?

You don't say whether your colleague is a him or a her and it makes little difference – but I'll plump for him, simply to avoid laborious he-she-or-them contortions.

You're right to tread carefully. However well meant your intervention, you could well appear insensitive. Never be surprised when people in deep grief fail to behave normally – or even rationally.

Which of his colleagues is closest to him? If it's you, then take on the task yourself. But if it's not, then avoid raising the subject with him directly: he could easily think you a busybody. The best person to make the initial approach is the person he most trusts. They may still be rebuffed but no lasting harm will have been done.

The chances are, however, that – to the right person, at the right time – he'll welcome the chance to open up a little. I've known at least two people in deep bereavement whose withdrawn behaviour severely discouraged any form of exchange – but who later revealed how isolated they'd been made to feel and how much they resented it. I know: not altogether reasonable; but that's the way it can be.

Finding the right words is extremely difficult. It's usually a great mistake to suggest that you know how they feel: you almost certainly don't. And even if you did, he'd find the suggestion offensive. Grief is an intensely personal emotion and those in its thrall know their pain to be unique.

For the opening approach, the slightest of prompts is the best idea. He'll know what's in your mind, almost before a word is spoken. And his response will be your best guide as to what to say next. Be happy to listen – endlessly. Above all, avoid the 'time-heals-everything' line of cheerful reassurance. Although it may, the way he feels now makes it unimaginable.

And finally, watch out for your own rising levels of impatience. As he talks and you listen, over the coming weeks or even months, you'll begin to wonder if his original perfectly genuine grief may not have matured into consuming self-pity. Could he even be *enjoying* his grief in some unlovely way?

Well – it may seem so. And there may even be some truth in it. But the phase will pass. Resist the temptation to shake him by the shoulders. Nobody gets through a bereavement more quickly because they've been instructed to pull themselves together.

I was forced to resign as finance director of a small manufacturer because I disagreed with the way the owner was running the business. One of its suppliers offered me a six-month contract to review their financial processes. Since then opportunities, however seemingly promising, have come to nothing. I'm now told my former employer is giving me unenthusiastic references. What should I do?

Don't let suspicion eat away at you: start by trying to establish the truth. If someone has told you that your former employer is slagging you off in his references, then that same someone should be able to get hold of a copy. And if it contains lies or demonstrably misleading implications, then at least you know your suspicions are well founded. Until that time, you must continue to entertain the possibility that you're just having a run of rotten luck.

If the evidence is there, go back to the supplier you did the financial review for. He may be in an invidious position himself – but show him the reference and ask him if he thinks it's full and fair. If he agrees that it's not, ask him a final favour: when next a promising opportunity presents itself, is he prepared to have an off-the-record word with your new prospect?

I expect you've also considered deleting all references to your time with the small manufacturer from your CV – but that might raise more questions than it answered.

Only if your former employer's references are clearly damaging should you knock on your lawyer's door. Above all, make heroic attempts to avoid exuding bitterness: bitter people interview extremely badly.

3 | *Being the boss*

- **Acting the part, doing the business**
- **Difficult decisions**
- **Managing the boss**

Some people – though perhaps luckily, not very many – seem born to be bosses. They spring from the womb fully equipped with vision, authority, an enviable sense of certainty and a thick skin.

Most of us find it more difficult. Becoming a boss, particularly as the result of internal promotion, can present huge personal problems. I once found myself the boss of a man I'd recently worked for and much admired. I never got it quite right.

New bosses are often very self-conscious; probably more aware of their new status than any of their colleagues, and torn between wanting to remain one of the gang and needing to establish a certain distance from them. You can't do both.

New bosses may also shrink from making difficult decisions. After years of feeling free to criticize authority, it's not always easy to exercise it oneself. The first time I knew I had to sack someone, I postponed the occasion for a shamefully long time; then conducted the interview with such extreme sensitivity that he left my office convinced I'd given him a resounding vote of confidence. Three weeks later, I had to start again – this time more successfully.

Analysing the problems presented under this heading, it's impossible not to conclude that however much good bosses may be paid they're probably worth it. Daily confronted with difficult decisions, facing the certainty of unpopularity from one quarter or another, deprived (quite often) of trustworthy confidants, it can, indeed, be lonely at the top; or even halfway up.

Acting the part, doing the business

I have just been made up to the board and do not want colleagues to think I've got superior by leaving the Christmas party too early but, equally, they'll probably let their hair down more once I've gone. The etiquette is all new to me. What's the best course of action?

Over the years, presumably, when you were younger and just one of the boys, you must have witnessed other new directors facing up to the same predicament. Can you remember how they did it?

My bet is you can't – because it's not nearly as defining a moment as you think. You imagine all eyes will be on you because you're acutely conscious of your new and exalted position. Well – they won't be. You're right, of course, to give it some thought; but you'd be wrong (and overly self-important) to agonize about it.

Test yourself against these two extremes: 'Just because I'm now a director, don't think I can't get as pissed as the rest of you'; and, 'As I'm sure you must realize, it would be most unseemly for someone of my seniority to become in any way ribald.' You don't need me to tell you to avoid both. Forget about etiquette, behave naturally, and aim for a reasonably early night. That should see you safely home.

A member of my sales team accidentally forwarded an e-mail to me that had already been around the office. It included comments from him and others that I was a poor team leader and not a patch on my predecessor. Everyone knows I received the e-mail, and they all know I know. Should I call a team meeting and get it all out in the open, or soldier on and pretend it never happened?

To give you a definitive answer to this extremely sensitive question, I would need to know a couple of things which I don't; and you may not, either.

The things are these. Being as dispassionate as you can, how much truth do you think that e-mail contained? And secondly: if you're prepared to acknowledge that you haven't made the greatest of starts in this job, how confident are you that, with a little more time, you'll be able to show them all?

If your confidence is high, then you could soon be starring for one of moviedom's favourite plots. New boss/captain/headmaster arrives; makes a poor start; not helped by bolshie underlings who miss much respected predecessor; critical opportunity/threat materializes; underlings baffled; through masterstroke, new leader confounds competitors and delivers goods. Team totally converted, buy flowers/drinks for new leader, tears all round.

In other words, a bad start can always be turned into triumph. But you'll need the opportunity – and the confidence and the ability to take advantage of it.

If you decide to give this route a go, then avoid any kind of showdown: you'll just sink lower still in their esteem. They'll never respond to reproach or argument: only performance.

But if your confidence is low, then you should probably look to make a fresh start somewhere else.

Four months ago, we took on an 'Oxford graduate' with an excellent CV. His work and attitude have so far been impressive but I recently bumped into one of his ex-college mates who says he dropped out in his second year. It makes me wonder what else he's been lying about. How do we handle this?

Clear the air just as soon as possible; don't let it fester.

The first thing to do is check the records. It would be disastrous if you were to act on the old mate's word only to discover that he'd got it wrong.

If the records confirm that your newcomer has lied, take him out to lunch – or out of the office, anyway. Make it as relaxed and unthreatening as you can. Tell him you're extremely pleased with the start he's made; then ask him, as if out of curiosity, why he felt he had to lie on his application form.

His response will almost certainly tell you all you need to know about him.

My guess is that you'll be greatly reassured – but even if you are, don't leave it at that. Tell him that you'll be writing him a strictly confidential letter, for the record but with copies to no one, making it clear that if he ever tells another lie, he's out. It may sound harsh – but it's in both your best interests. And it means you can keep the incident to yourself without being irresponsible.

I have just taken one of the hardest decisions of my working life and made three of my middle managers redundant. My secretary now tells me that one, who is forty-nine and has been with the company for years, hasn't told his wife. By all accounts, he continues to 'go to work' as usual. This probably isn't my problem but I do feel responsible. What should I do?

It may not be your problem but you're right to feel you can't ignore it. Nor can you delegate – you've got to talk to him yourself. Since you can't – or shouldn't – ring him at home, you need to find out where he goes every day. By the sound of it, your secretary may know.

Then arrange to bump into him. If necessary (to protect your secretary) you may have to pretend that the meeting is by chance – it doesn't really matter if he doesn't believe you. Don't pussyfoot around too much: just ask, does your wife know?

My guess is that he's already regretting his deception but finding it harder and harder with every day that passes to think of a way out of it. If he couldn't bring himself to tell his wife when he first lost his job, it must be hideously more difficult now.

So by far the best thing you can do to help is give him a new opportunity to come clean. Say you'll give him a letter with the current date on it – explaining as sensitively as possible why he's being made redundant. Write it for his wife's eyes as much as his. Then sign him up with an out-placement firm (which you probably should have done earlier). I know it's deception – but the man must be in turmoil and you've got to help him. Nobody else can.

We have recently appointed a new sales executive who came complete with a glowing reference from his previous employer. The problem is, he doesn't live up to his credentials and I suspect that the glowing reference was written on purpose to encourage me to take a very average employee off the previous employer's hands. Do I have any grounds for challenging the previous employer to take his employee back?

I expect you've written a few references yourself in your time so you really ought to know by now how to interpret them. Always aim off for the author's motives: they may spring from compassion, guilt or even – occasionally – a malign interest in disabling a competitor, but the net effect is the same. The great majority of references overpraise and undercriticize.

Always look for what isn't there. Not a word about reliability: why not? Learn how to decode hidden messages: 'an effective if sometimes unconventional approach with customers' means he's screwed up as many sales leads as he's secured.

I imagine you're joking when you suggest that you have grounds for insisting that his previous employer takes him back? Not a chance.

If he's a real no-hoper, swallow your pride and give him notice: the sooner the better for both of you. And if he asks you for a reference, I imagine you'll craft it with unusual care.

I want to take on a graduate trainee and have a pile of applications, which all seem good on paper. The obvious thing would be to interview them but I am rushed off my feet. I could entrust the task to one of my managers but I'm worried in case they choose the wrong person. What should I do?

Well, fancy. Seldom has the description of a problem more clearly contained the evidence of its cause. Why do you suppose you're rushed off your feet? Might it just have something to do with the fact that you don't trust your managers to manage?

And who picked them, by the way? If it was you, why did you pick people you now don't trust to pick people?

Take a deep breath – and start teaching yourself to trust. You'll hate it to start with, and the Almighty will certainly come up with a couple of early disasters to test your resolve; but it will soon get better, I promise.

On the graduate trainee: you should ask your managers to interview them all – each candidate to be seen by two managers – and to agree between themselves on a short list of three. These are the only ones you see. You and your managers then confer and agree on the lucky winner. In the event of a split, the casting vote is yours.

An important bonus: because your managers have been actively involved in the selection process, they will want to help their choice be successful.

Come on, now. I'm sure you can do it. Why not start on Monday?

It has been brought to my attention that a few of my staff are downloading Internet porn when they should be working. I think it is a serious problem but I don't know what action to take. Can you advise me?

I wonder who it was who brought this to your attention?

And I wonder a bit about the underlying reasons for your concern. Do you disapprove of porn, or of people enjoying themselves, or of people wasting company time? Try and sort it out in your own mind before proceeding much further.

The area is a hugely complex one – and getting more so. Some companies have fired employees for using company networks to obtain pornography. Others have started monitoring the websites being accessed by staff – and even their e-mails. But you need to be careful: you may be getting yourself into personal privacy issues here.

The best idea seems to be to produce a short Code of Conduct, integrated into your standard terms of employment, so that misuse of the Internet becomes a recognized disciplinary offence. The most important paragraph should simply state that company equipment may be used for company purposes only. All employees with access to the Internet should be asked to sign and return a copy.

For advice on useful software packages available, try CenturyCom on 01635 295500: they're said to be knowledgeable and helpful.

Alternatively, you might just let it be be known that, in order to guard against Internet-borne viruses, daily random monitoring will take place with immediate effect. This is a bit like installing speed-cameras with no film in them: they flash convincingly, deter the wrongdoer and don't cost much.

A very popular member of my team is not pulling his weight. I have spoken with him about it informally but may now need to caution him. I am worried about how well this will go down with other team members and how it may impact on my authority.

I'm sure you know exactly what this slimy charmer is up to, but just in case you don't, I'll tell you.

He's playing you at poker: pitting his popularity against your authority. I bet he did it at school, too. He was the good-looking one at the back of the class who gave the trainee French teacher such a miserable time.

He likes to challenge you in front of others, doesn't he? And every time he gets away with it, and is seen to get away with it, his hand grows stronger and yours weaker.

It's the attitude of the other team members that's the clue here. As long as he continues to out-bluff you, they'll go on thinking he's wonderful. I know it's not very grown-up of them, particularly since they're presumably suffering from his indolence, but it's human. So you've got to break the pattern.

And here you're in a much stronger position than the trainee French teacher. She couldn't sack him. You can.

Consult your company secretary or lawyer or HR director; then give him a written warning and a specified date for the next review.

Forget about popularity: that's his game. Restore your authority: that's yours.

One of my managers is a bit of a last-minuter and I worry that he covers up things he hasn't done and this could have a bad effect on my business. Do I challenge him and, if so, how? I don't want to undermine his authority with the rest of my staff or hassle him unnecessarily.

Why, I wonder, are you so diffident about this? If you have good reason to suspect him of serial incompetence, then you must certainly do something about it.

In fact, I bet I know the answer to my own question. I bet you pride yourself on running a really friendly, informal company. I bet you talk about family atmosphere and how everyone's got an equal voice and how all doors are open all the time and how it's up to people what hours they work as long as the job gets done. Well, some of this is fine: but it also means that you feel inhibited from having a perfectly reasonable word with your manager because it might seem a 'challenge'.

That's the trouble with folksy business cultures: they can all too easily deter leaders from exerting a bit of necessary discipline and encourage the chronically sloppy to carry on slopping.

So if you haven't introduced a programme of regular performance reviews, you should do now.

If your entire staff knows that, say every six months, their performance is going to be formally assessed, then it's a great deal easier to be straight with them – while still maintaining a perfectly friendly atmosphere.

By applying the programme to everyone, and by making it unfailingly regular, you can voice dissatisfaction early – and without it taking on quite such personal and disproportionate significance.

Your manager may not be quite as fond of you in the future; but if you can't live with that, you shouldn't be in charge.

I manage a small team in a publishing company and we all work very hard to get things done on time with limited resources. We have recently taken on a young but very talented work experience girl who has been helping certain members of the team on various projects. The difficulty is that the other team members feel shortchanged because she hasn't been allocated to them. It's rare for us to find talented volunteers to help in the office, so finding another intern is not an option. Is there anything I can do to ease the tensions in the office?

What's needed here, by the sound of it, is a bit of leavening. If the girl's on work experience, she won't be with you for very much longer – but you can certainly help the situation immediately simply by recognizing it.

Next Friday evening (or whenever seems suitable) gather your managers and the intern around you for a glass of wine and explain that she's been so efficient and helpful and productive that everyone now wants a piece of her but that's impossible. So from now on her time will be allocated in the only truly equitable manner: by weekly lottery. Hold the first draw there and then – and then have another glass of wine.

Don't forget to take the girl into your confidence before you announce all this. She's likely to find it quite flattering but don't let it come as a surprise.

Difficult decisions

I have recently been made the head of my department, having spent several years as one of its members, and am finding it difficult to impose my authority. I know I am going to have to fire some of my former colleagues to reduce the overhead and the idea of doing it keeps me awake at night. Am I in over my head?

Everybody who's ever been promoted from within has faced this problem. Only right bastards enjoy it, and you clearly aren't one.

Hang on to that word 'recently': because it will soon get better. Meanwhile, try two things.

First: try to imagine what it's like to be your colleagues. They know perfectly well that you can't go on being one of the boys for ever but they're not going to make it easy for you. Why should they – you're the one who got the nod. But it will be as much a relief for them as for you when the new relationship settles down. Which it will.

Second: try to pretend that you've been brought in from outside. Make your judgements on facts and observation: not sentiment.

Nothing will make firing colleagues easy or pleasant – but don't expect sympathy. However much you hate it all, be very, very generous with your time. You may think the first conversation will be the worst, but it won't be. They'll go away and talk and have a drink and tell their family and then they'll think how unfair it all is and the resentment will bubble up and that's when you must talk again. And when you must listen . . . and listen . . . and listen.

And whatever you do, don't blame someone else further up the line. Don't pretend that had it been left to you, it would never have happened. That's the quickest way to lose both old friends and new respect.

I set up a printing business two years ago, and desperately need a loan to keep up with rapid expansion. No bank will give me another loan, but my father-in-law has offered me one. On the one hand it's a great offer, on the other I'm uneasy about accepting it. We've never had a good relationship and he made it clear how foolish he thought I was to leave my job in the City and set up alone. I'm worried what sort of emotional pressure he'll try to bring to bear if I accept his offer.

You're absolutely right to feel uneasy. If it weren't for your understandable desperation to keep your business afloat, I'm fairly certain you'd have declined his offer already.

Just run over the facts as you've given them to me. He and you don't get on that well. He disapproved of your setting up the business in the first place. No bank will grant you a further loan – which, even allowing for bankers' traditional caution, presumably means you're pretty thinly stretched already. And on top of all that, you should assume that we're in for an economic downturn which could well affect the printing trade.

Wherever it comes from, that loan will be at risk. It will be bad enough for you if your business goes down. But if it goes down taking a sizeable chunk of your father-in-law's life savings, it will put your wife in an intolerable position and your misery will be twice compounded.

So, tempting though his offer will continue to be, please close your mind to it. Try other banks – if your order book really does look that good, you should have a story to tell. Talk to other, competitive printers about the possibility of merging or cost-sharing. Advertise for a working or sleeping partner with available capital. Just make sure that everything is done on a strictly business basis. And keep the family well out of it.

There are two candidates left for the top job in one of my company's most important divisions. Both, a man and a woman, are in their mid-thirties and capable. I am worried the woman is likely to want a baby in the next few years and require a substantial amount of time off. But I am also keen to promote a woman; we have so few in the company. What is the best way forward?

Now you know why you get paid so much. You're faced with an extremely difficult decision, made all the more so because, whichever one you go for, there will be those who think you've been influenced by prejudice. Since you can't avoid such suspicion, you must satisfy yourself, if nobody else, that you haven't. My best advice is that you should go through a few systematic checks – then trust to God and instinct.

Check One: pretend to yourself that the woman isn't a woman; so you can ignore the possibility she may need time off. Which of the two would you choose then? Is it still a dead heat?

Check Two: forget you are keen to promote women. If you already had an equal number of men and women in senior positions, which of the two would you choose?

Check Three: analyse their management styles. Are they good at setting long-term goals and letting people get on with it? Or do they need to be around to be effective? If you're right about her wanting children, this will help you determine how serious, if at all, the occasional absences might be.

Check Four: stop thinking about the immediate effect of the choice. Whatever you decide, it will be unpopular in some quarters so don't let your worries about that influence your decision. Think two years down the line: under either leader, how successful will the division be? That is what you'll be judged on, nothing else.

You should now be quite a bit clearer in your head. With any luck, you will wake up one morning quite soon and find that, by some mysterious process, you've come to a decision.

A last tip: once the decision is made, you will be faced with one easy conversation and one difficult one. When passing on the bad news, you must absolutely resist the temptation to soften the blow; to imply that if she had been a man, or if he had been a woman, it could so easily have gone the other way. You must assure them both that you simply set out to pick the better person for the job. And you will only be able to say that with conviction if you have.

One of our senior managers has told me that they are intending to undergo cosmetic surgery, and asked whether the two-day hospital stay and fourteen-day recovery time will be considered as sick leave or holiday. We do not have a company policy established for this situation! What do you think?

Only you will know this person's history. But if (and I'm risking feminist wrath here, but it's statistically more likely that she's a woman) – if she's a conscientious individual with no previous record of dreaming up work-shirking ruses, then you should follow your instinct and consider it sick-leave.

She is, after all, going to undergo an operation; and will certainly need recovery time. It's only the fact that the decision to subject herself to surgery is a voluntary one that raises any element of doubt in your mind.

If I were you, I'd try to forget the word 'cosmetic'. It smacks too much of vanity and frivolity – as if someone's demanding an extra week off to top up their suntan.

But, as always, do think through the consequences. You're setting a precedent – and though you may never receive an equivalent request again, you'd better be clear in your own mind what the company policy now is.

Time off for tattooing, for example? Or navel-piercing?

Christmas and New Year are one of my office's busiest times but naturally most people want time off. What do you think is the fairest way of choosing who has to work?

Start (if you haven't already) by working out what is the mini-mum number of staff you'll need. And think not just about overall numbers but specific functions. For example, you might be able to do without back-office people for a day or two, but not without those who deal with customers.

Then be sure you know your own plans. I assume you're happy to work over this period yourself? If not, your problem will become even more acute.

Finally, don't hope to make money over those few days: decide that the limit of your ambition is to impress the hell out of your customers and get up the noses of your competition. So see it as an investment period – and steel yourself to the fact that it's going to cost you.

Once you've got that clear in your head, you can take your people into your confidence. Tell them that you've got to be open for business; that you're determined to do it well; and that, ideally, nobody should be working against their will or if there are strong family reasons for them to be at home.

Then ask for volunteers. Establish who is totally against work-ing and why. Devise an extremely generous bonus pool. Be imaginative. Think not just about your employees but their families. For example, don't just dish out money but offer other options. Ask them what their families would appreciate: such as a weekend for two in Paris in the spring, all expenses paid including a babysitter; or a Center Parcs weekend for the whole family. In other words, make it just that little bit easier for your members of staff to break the unwelcome news at home.

This may not solve all your problems – but at least it should minimize threats, instructions and general disgruntlement.

My PA had several weeks off after her mother died about four months ago. But since her return, she has not been concentrating on her work. Embarrassing omissions have occurred. I want to be sympathetic but, as MD, I can't afford for something disastrous to happen. We've discussed her attitude but she just seems to get upset or lose her temper. What should I do?

I feel extremely sorry for both of you. If there was a perfect (and perfectly humane) solution to this predicament you'd almost certainly have thought of it yourself – but there isn't.

She was once, presumably, extremely efficient and reliable? If so, it's an odds-on bet that she will be again, but it will take time. When overcoming grief, four months is not long – though it probably feels like a lifetime to you.

So you must make one steely-hearted decision right now: stop taking chances with your business. If one of her 'embarrassing omissions' turned out to be catastrophic, it would not only be bad news for you and all your other employees; it would also make it infinitely more difficult for confidence to be restored in the future. I promise you: it's in her best interest as well as in yours to see that she's not exposed to this risk. So from now on, concentrate all your energy and imagination not on what to do but on how to do it.

If you know any members of her family, you must talk to one of them. They'll have noticed some changes as well – and are far more likely to be sympathetic and helpful if you put the position to them squarely.

Then talk to her. This time, don't dwell on her shortcomings: she'll only get tearful and defensive again. Tell her that you value her so much that you're moving her into a less demanding job – on the same salary – until she's her old self again. Make it clear, in the gentlest possible way, that this decision is not open to negotiation.

I realize that this is an expensive suggestion; but if you really rate her, then it's surely worth it. If you don't, of course, you'll have to bite an even more distasteful bullet.

I have ten trainees but only seven jobs. Six trainees are clear contenders. Of the remaining four, one is black and, though my company has no specific policy of positive discrimination and the trainee is no better (and possibly slightly less qualified) than the others, I am inclined to make him an offer. Is this the right thing to do?

How big, I wonder, is the gap between the six who are clear contenders and the other four? I ask because it's just possible, if the gap is great, that you shouldn't be taking on any of them but should rather be looking outside to fill the seventh place.

If you still believe that taking any one of the four would be a responsible decision, then I think your instinct is right. However much you and he might wish otherwise, your black candidate – all other things being equal – would almost certainly find it harder to get another job. To be one of only three who fail to make the grade would be an even more bitter experience for him than for the other two.

But do be as sure as you can that he's got a reasonable chance of making good. You'll do him no favours by inviting him to do a job while harbouring doubts about his ability to do it.

Failure for members of minorities is doubly cruel. If a white, middle-class male doesn't make it, that's life. But if a black (or a woman) doesn't make it, it confirms the bigots in their views of an entire category. So please be very careful with this man.

The finance director of my company has been stealing significant sums from petty cash. I have proof that it is her, but I'm not sure how to deal with the situation. I can even sympathize with her – she is bringing up two children on her own and is struggling with large debts left by her ex-husband. She happens to be excellent at her job, and fits in very well with the rest of the team, and I'm not sure that I want to lose her.

You have proof that a trusted director is a criminal yet you're keeping it to yourself. This makes you an accessory.

Sooner rather than later, someone else will rumble her – one of her staff, an auditor, another director. You may have convinced yourself that you're protecting her, but in fact you're exposing her to the most hideous risk. Once her crime becomes public knowledge, she'll have to be fired. And for a financial director, who's also a single parent with heavy debts, the consequences would be quite appalling. Her only hope of an equivalent job would be to lie her way into it.

So deciding to act is the easy bit: you have no choice. Working out exactly how to do it is more difficult.

Start by defining your ideal outcome. It sounds as if you'd like to keep her – but you can only do that if she pays back the money and stays straight.

Pick a Friday afternoon: she'll need the weekend to collect her thoughts. Tell her you know everything, tell her you rate her, tell her you trust her, tell her you want her to stay. If you think she deserves it, up her pay a little. Offer her legal help: she should be getting more support from that ex-husband of hers. Present her with a long-term repayment plan. And make it absolutely clear that there can be no second chances.

Put it all in writing, confide in at least one of your boardroom colleagues (preferably your chairman), lodge the letters with your lawyer – and hope.

If it all comes out later – and you should assume it will – then you will be seen to have acted both compassionately and responsibly. But do please act soon.

It's been obvious for a while that two of my employees really don't get on, and that one of them is frequently made very upset by the other. I don't want to lose either of them as employees, but I'm not sure how to deal with the situation.

Try this. Get them both together – maybe over a drink or a meal – and then invite them to sort it out themselves.

Don't favour one over the other. Don't attempt to allocate blame or even suggest a solution. Don't labour the point. Just say that it's obvious to all that there's friction between them; that it's affecting their work; that you value them both; and that you trust them as intelligent beings to resolve the problem sensibly. Give them a month to come back to you. Resist the temptation to add, 'or otherwise I'll have to deal with it myself'. If they're halfway bright, they'll know that anyway.

It's astonishing how often this simple technique works. It may sound risky, but it's not.

If it fails – if one of them turns out to be resistant and obstructive, insisting that the fault lies entirely with the other – then you'll know far more clearly what needs to be done.

But there's a very good chance that the challenge of being their own managers will appeal to them both. Who knows: they might even get to respect each other.

Managing the boss

My boss has hired his daughter to work with me as a deputy. She isn't good at the job, and at twenty-three she has no relevant experience and no particular qualifications to be doing what she's doing. Her salary is ridiculously high for someone her age, and it's coming out of my budget. On top of all of that, I constantly have to drop what I'm doing to sort out her problems with what she's doing. Should I say something to my boss?

Does your boss have a boss or is he also the proprietor? Because what you describe is the sort of cosy little set-up much favoured by family businesses: fine and dandy if you're family and a potential nightmare if you're not. So it seems to me likely that the problem of the daughter is not actually a daughter problem at all but a symptom of another, bigger problem – and one which you may well have been trying not to face up to.

The very best companies to work for, whether big or small, exude a strong and unspoken sense of impartiality. Just one set of rules that apply to everyone. Merit and contribution recognized equally from whatever source. No favouritism, no inner circles, no cronies, no cliques. Miraculously, some family businesses manage to maintain these demanding standards but many don't. So among non-family staff, there's always a lurking suspicion that they may not be playing on the levellest of playing fields. Your boss's action in imposing his daughter on you and your budget will certainly have confirmed you in this suspicion. From now on, it will infect even your smallest dissatisfaction – and it won't go away.

So I'm afraid you need to think of moving on. Once you've come to terms with this decision (and make sure that it *is* a decision: not just a watery sort of tentative possible future option) go to your boss and tell him that you're planning to go and exactly why. Don't make your reason daughter-specific: it would sound too petty and besides it isn't. Paint the truer, broader picture.

If he's ever going to change his ways, now's his chance. But I doubt if he'll take it.

My boss keeps borrowing money off me (a pound here, £5 there), because he's 'not got to the bank' or he's 'come out without his wallet' at the pub at lunchtime. Then he fails to pay me back. I don't want to put his back up yet feel I should say something – but what?

It's a long time since I heard of anybody borrowing a pound. What does he do with a pound, I wonder? Serious borrowers never touch anyone for less than a tenner, so maybe you've got something to be thankful for.

But it all adds up and I can quite see why you're a bit narked. By the sound of it, you don't put it down to forgetfulness, either – and seniors consistently failing to pay back juniors smacks of the worst kind of abuse of power.

All I've got to go on in building up a character portrait of your boss is a man who systematically borrows insultingly small sums from his subordinates and then chooses not to pay them back. This makes me wonder whether you shouldn't trade him in.

But if, by chance, he enjoys some redeeming features, such as training you well and providing you with guidance and support, then you have a choice. You can treat your loans as a sort of apprenticeship fee: the cost of getting a decent training that will pay off later. In other words, keep handing over the loot but stop expecting to see it back. Or you can start keeping a notebook.

Make sure everybody knows you're keeping a notebook. Use it to record telephone numbers, humorous anecdotes, petty wagers – and loans. Next time he touches you for a fiver, pull out the book and jot down the date and the amount before you hand it over. Then wait till the end of the month and send in a detailed invoice. But if I were you, I'd go for the apprenticeship option.

4 | *Whose side am I on? Conflicting loyalties*

You can always tell when a company is badly led or is otherwise going through a rocky patch. All sense of competition, instead of being outwardly directed, turns inwards. Baronies spring up; job satisfaction is derived not from beating the living daylights out of market competitors but by outwitting a rival baron just along the passage.

One inevitable consequence of such turf wars is that staff members – and often reasonably lowly ones – get helplessly caught up and find themselves tugged in conflicting directions. When irreconcilable demands for exclusive commitment come from two or more senior people, the pressure on the individual can become intolerable. In the absence of a boss to appeal to – since the boss will almost certainly be one of the barons – good people often decide to leave the company altogether; and so the downward spiral continues.

Common, too, is the conflict between loyalty to friend and loyalty to company. At the trivial level, it's seldom a problem; if she goes to a hen party that sees the dawn in, then you cover for the friend. Of course.

But what do you do – and it's likely to creep up on you almost imperceptibly – when you come to realize that the occasional lapse has become habitual? That's a great deal harder to deal with. If you're halfway human, you'll be tempted to procrastinate; to put off any action on the grounds that – somehow, some day soon – it will miraculously sort itself. But it won't, I'm afraid; it's a lot more likely to blow up in your face.

My boss has a drink problem and I am increasingly having to cover up for him. I don't wish to be disloyal but I do find the situation difficult and am worried that the lies I keep telling on his behalf will somehow rebound on me.

Covering up for colleagues is one of the great and joyous parts of belonging. We did it at school to foil the teachers – and we do it willingly at work to show solidarity and friendship. Where it goes wrong – and it's certainly going wrong for you – is when it becomes habitual.

To cover the occasional indulgent lunch is one thing. Maintaining a smokescreen around continual underperformance is quite another. What's more, there comes a point – and you've reached it – when you're doing no one a favour, not even your boss.

So first make the decision that you've got to stop the subterfuge; and then begin to work out how. I'm sure you must start by trying to talk to him. It will certainly be difficult and it may not work; but he'll never forgive you, and perhaps rightly, if you haven't tried. Make sure he understands that you've got to end the cover-up and why.

After that, you're into what you call disloyalty – but that's being too harsh on yourself. There's nothing disloyal about trying to stop a person screwing up his life. Don't confuse it with sneaking: it isn't.

Who you talk to next depends on who's available, who you know best and who you trust. The personnel director? The company doctor? A friend of his? His family? But you've got to talk to someone – and what's more, it must be someone with whom you can properly leave the responsibility.

I am MD of a high-growth company recently acquired by a multinational. Our new parent has told us to use its 'big six' firm of accountants and not our existing firm, which has served us well for years and was a great support through the acquisition. Our parent has praised their work but wants to standardize. I am not happy but don't see how I can simply say no.

Your question, of course, will come with a sickening sense of familiarity to a great many excellent accountancy firms who happen not to be members of the big six. And, for that matter, to thousands of other service companies whose long-standing and valued clients suddenly find themselves under instruction from new corporate masters to standardize, harmonize, rational-ize – in other words, terminate – hitherto entirely satisfactory professional relationships.

It's a wrenching business, often involving those who have

become friends as well as advisers. It's also extremely difficult to know where good business sense stops and sentimentality takes over.

You're quite right to question your freedom simply to say no. You can't. Much of the (often spurious) justification for acquisition centres round centralization and cost-saving. And there are real and powerful reasons for a multinational wanting its accounts to be audited by a single firm.

There are just two approaches you could try which – quite legitimately – might preserve at least part of your business with your existing firm.

If there is any element of their service which applies to your particular sector or region – and *only* to your particular sector or region – then you have good reason to argue the commercial case for retaining local knowledge and past experience.

To which you can add the appeal of comparison. However compelling the argument for the seamless, worldwide application of the mega-firm's armies, even the mightiest of CEOs dislikes feeling held to ransom by a monopoly supplier. The opportunity for a little side-by-side assessment, even if only on a limited scale, can often be seen as a cost-effective way of keeping the mega-firm on its toes.

Try it, anyway. Your existing firm will certainly be grateful. But if their senior partner is your daughter's godfather, say a sorrowful goodbye immediately. Your new corporate parent will never believe your motives.

I've been promoted internally and my new boss wants me to start immediately, but I need at least a month to tie up loose ends in my current position. My present boss would also prefer me to stay and get things finished off before I move on. I want to stay on good terms with both of them, so what is my best course of action?

This may be temperamentally very difficult for you – but what you must do, just for one month, is abandon your favoured working routines and set out to achieve the impossible.

It's clear from your need for 'at least a month to tie up loose ends' that you're a conscientious person, used to an orderly way of doing things. When you can finally put your current job behind you and commit yourself totally to the new one, you can always return to such methodical ways. But for now, you've got to do two full-time jobs to the full satisfaction of two bosses. And you can.

It will play hell with your private life, your sleep, your sense of self-control and your digestion. You'll have to work out ingenious ways of doing things and find little chinks of time you never knew existed. Your evenings and weekends will be grievously invaded and you'll face the wooden disapproval of friends and loved ones.

But it's only for a month; you'll be amazed at your own productivity; and you'll be extremely pleased with yourself when you've pulled it off.

I recently recommended an acquaintance for a vacancy at work, and was pleased when he was offered the job. But now I sorely regret having recommended him. He is unreliable, is mouthy with the boss, and rude to other colleagues. I know from their pointed comments that they blame me for his appointment, and feel I should say something to him. I don't think I know him well enough for this sort of showdown, but feel I ought to do something.

I don't want to rub it in – but just in case you're ever inclined to be quite as idiotic again, you'd better square up to what you did this time. You recommended an acquaintance – an *acquaintance*! – for a job in your own company; and not even a close acquaintance at that but someone, in your own words, you don't know well enough to have a heart-to-heart with.

What, I wonder, were you thinking of? It sounds to me as if you're rather too anxious to be liked – and are now experiencing the inevitable, ironical consequence: the extreme disfavour of your colleagues.

Sorry about all that, but it had to be said. Now for a bit of recovery work.

Your best hope is that your boorish acquaintance gets himself fired as soon as possible. From what you say, he's setting about this objective with skill and determination. The fact that he's unreliable and mouthy with the boss is the only good news in your letter. Long may it last.

But you do have to speak to him. Not, I think, a long rehearsal of his faults and flaws coupled with an impassioned plea for reform: it wouldn't work, and anyway, you don't even want it to. Just tell him as briefly as possible that you now regret having recommended him and that he should no longer assume that he enjoys your support. Avoid elaboration if at all possible.

The next bit's more tricky; but somehow you've got to make sure that your boss knows how you now feel without coming across as a treacherous shit. I suggest a short note, which simply says, in toto, 'I would like you to know that I yesterday told [*boorish acquaintance*] that I now regret having recommended him to you.'

The sooner he's fired, of course, the fewer legal problems there'll be: so don't hang around.

I founded my own business ten years ago. I now employ sixty people and want to reduce the hours I put in. How do you work part-time without the business suffering?

The worst thing you can do is try to reduce your hours without redefining your role.

You founded your own business – and you clearly still see it as your own business. I notice you use the first person singular, 'I now employ sixty people.' You seem to want to hang on to that sense of authorship and ownership – while having more time to yourself. Well, you may be able to; but it's very, very difficult and can be extremely unfair on the others in the company. And if that's how they see it, the business will certainly suffer.

I sense from the way you put the question that you haven't yet invited any of those sixty people to have a share in the business. If that's the case, then it's time to think about that, too.

Go away for a few days (with a friendly outside adviser if you know one) and work out how you would like the business run. Your starting point should be a non-negotiable condition: *you must base your plan on the assumption that you will have left the company altogether.*

Do you have a natural leader on your staff at the moment? And notice that I say 'a natural leader', not 'a natural successor to you'. First generation managers are notoriously bad at picking successors, not least because the necessary qualities are so different. You need a good leader – not a pale replica of you.

If you don't have the talent internally, acknowledge that you'll need to look outside. At all costs, resist the temptation to say, 'Well, I could do that myself – at least for the time being.' Stick to the rule: this company has got to be run successfully – *with absolutely no contribution from you.*

If you fail to identify a leader, you must postpone any thought of easing off until you have. But make yourself a deadline for finding one – and stick to it; otherwise you'll drift indefinitely.

When you've found your leader, take them into your confidence. Start by giving them a share of the company. You may find this painful – but it's the only way. Then, between you, go over your plans and see if you agree.

Only then should you say to your new leader, 'Right. You're in charge. I'd be happy to put in some hours a week – but it's your call. You must decide where I could be useful.'

And if you find all this too wrenching to contemplate, you should probably go on working full-time for a bit longer.

I need to hire an outside agency to do some advertising work for me. I have identified the best candidate, but the person who would be handling the account is a friend of mine. I've always thought it was best to avoid working with friends, and I'm not sure whether to go ahead and ask him to do it.

By the best candidate, I assume you mean the best agency. And if it really is the best agency, then it should certainly house more than one person qualified to handle your account. One-man bands are dodgy; and if the one man is a friend, they're doubly so.

Getting the work you want out of an advertising agency is not always easy. You may find them slow; they may think you're too unadventurous. Deadlines may come and go; fierce disputes about matters of subjective judgement are to be expected; tears and tantrums are not unknown. There may well come a time when you need to put your business up for review. So your instinct is right: you'll find it very much easier to weather all this if you and your account handler have an agreeable but exclusively professional relationship.

Your friend can still be useful, though. Explain your reasons – then use him as an unofficial adviser on agency/client relationships. Ask for guidance if you're not sure whether to use stick or carrot. That way, even if you finally need to move your business, your friendship can still survive.

I'm a non-executive director of a small retail group that's going through a rocky period financially. The company director, whom

I know well, recently confided in me that he's been suffering from depression, and is seeking medical treatment. It's been going on for four weeks, but his performance at work is still noticeably under par, at a critical time for the company. Should I suggest that someone else might do a better job as director, at least until he's fully recovered?

It's going to be tough on both of you – but I bet you know exactly what you've got to do. Suppose, in the name of friendship, you decided to keep your worries to yourself and let him struggle on? The chances are that the company would lurch from bad to worse (with serious implications for everyone who works there); that increasing anxiety would compound your director's depression; and that you'd be as guilty as anyone when it ended in tears.

Non-executives are appointed precisely to take this sort of action. Use inhuman sensitivity. Lie if necessary to protect your man. See that he has access to all the help that he needs. Plan so that he can return in the event of recovery. But the sooner you act, the better for everyone. Sorry.

My boss is planning some radical reforms at work, which will affect the way we do business as well as individual job descriptions. As a senior manager, I'm privy to these confidential plans, but some of my staff know that something is up and have been asking me what's going on. I know that I shouldn't tell them the full story yet, but I feel I owe it to them to at least outline what might be happening – after all, it's their jobs that will be affected. What should I do?

You shouldn't really be asking. You're a senior manager who's been entrusted with confidential information in the belief that you'll keep it to yourself. And so you must: it's one of the boring conditions of being a prefect.

I can understand your unease – though I wonder a bit about your motives. You can't be a senior manager *and* one of the boys. You can't maintain the trust of your boss *and* leak secrets to your staff. You can't maintain respect without occasionally forfeiting affection.

Your thought of letting them in on an outline of the changes is about as silly an idea as you could have. In one blow, you'll betray a confidence, fuel further speculation – and almost certainly mislead your own staff. I'll bet you anything you like that the plans your boss has in mind will go on being modified until the very last minute.

All you can do is go to your boss; confirm (because he's bound to know anyway) that speculation is rife; and encourage him to go firm on an announcement date as soon as possible. Then get his agreement to make that date known.

Please forswear all other hints, half-truths and innuendoes. Implacable opacity is your only respectable option.

5 | *My brilliant career*

- **How am I doing? (And why won't they tell me?)**
- **Coping with change**
- **Left out of the loop**
- **How do I know when it's time to move on?**

However benign your company, however thoughtful your boss and attentive your HR department, no one is ever going to be as interested in your career as you are yourself. You should never be surprised, therefore, or unduly miffed, if you fail to get the regular appraisals (preferably favourable, naturally) that most people appreciate.

But many bosses are sloppy about providing feedback – and the luckless worker is left to guess: exactly what lies behind this creepy silence? Am I doing so well that I'm now taken for granted? Are they trying to tell me something but are too gutless to spell it out? Or are they just too preoccupied with their own lives to give a thought to mine?

This sort of uneasy speculation has a corrosive effect on confidence. And it's often the more talented ones who suffer from the greatest self-doubt and who crave the odd word of approval most intensely.

Another challenge to confidence is the prospect of change – particularly when the nature of that change is still enshrouded in rumour and gossip. Such uncertainty often induces an irrational attachment to the status quo. When plans are made known, and openly discussed and debated, our resistance to change diminishes sharply. Bosses please note.

And then: when to stay – and when to move on? I used to tell people that only when they'd been unhappy for at least six months, and only when they were fairly sure that a better job lay waiting, should they make that big decision to go. That's probably still right, but I speak with some diffidence. I joined a company when I was twenty-four, stayed with it until I was fifty-eight, then joined its parent company where I'm still to be found. So I'm no great expert on the risks and rewards of changing jobs.

How am I doing?
(And why won't they tell me?)

I don't get any feedback from my boss and find it very hard to gauge how I am doing. Although I've mentioned this to my boss, she remains non-committal and I still feel as though I'm working in a void. It's making me feel demotivated and I'm beginning to lose pride in my work. What can I do to resolve the situation?

It sounds as if you have good cause for concern here – but we need to be sure. It's just possible, you see (and don't get huffy now), that what you're actually longing for is not more feedback but more praise. When we say to others, 'I want you to be absolutely honest with me,' what we often mean is, 'Please tell me how wonderful I am.'

Presumably your boss has other people reporting to her; does she keep them starved of feedback, too? Or is it only you?

If it's only you, then you have a next-stage question to answer. Is she more reticent with you because, although your work is good, she has an irrational bias against you? Or is it because (at least in her eyes) you're not as good as the others? Try very hard to be honest with yourself.

If it's yes to either of the above, then the problem you have is particular to you. The fact that she remains non-committal could simply be reluctance on her part to come clean with you. (I know she should; but not all bosses can bring themselves to say hurtful things.) So be more upfront. Get her alone and say, 'I know you think my work inferior. Please don't worry about my feelings: am I right or wrong?' Put like that, her reaction will tell you all you need to know.

But if, after all this self-examination, you're still convinced that the problem is a general one, and lies less with you than with her, you must make another appeal. This time, do it formally but helpfully – and with one or more of your colleagues. Don't be reproachful – just make it clear that you'll all be happier and better motivated if you get regular feedback, good and bad. And suggest a starting date.

A colleague recently told me – confidentially – how much she was earning. I was surprised how high it was because she is at a similar age and level as me, but assumed I'd be brought up to a similar rate after my first pay review. Although my appraisal has been very positive, I've only been offered a measly pay increase. Could I get more if I tell my boss I know what my colleague earns? And should I break my colleague's confidence?

I'm very glad you've asked me all this before actually doing anything, otherwise you might have made several dogs' break-fasts out of your life.

Unless your company believes in grades – which it clearly doesn't – you should never assume that people of similar age and level will be earning precisely the same salary: there are far too many other factors at work. It's perfectly possible that your company had to pay a premium to attract this indiscreet colleague of yours; and few companies are saintly enough (or insane enough) to give their existing staff an automatic and equivalent rise in compensation.

It's also possible that your indiscreet colleague is being a little economical with the truth. Whatever the motive, people's inclination to flatter the size of their salary continues to amaze me. She may, of course, have simply wanted to wind you up; in which case she's certainly succeeded.

Work well, be patient, make sure of your facts. Then, politely, ask for more money. But under no circumstances refer to your colleague's notional salary.

My company has not been doing so well recently and I have applied for jobs elsewhere – but now it is rumoured that the company will soon start looking for voluntary redundancies. Should I put everything on hold and wait for a redundancy pay-out?

You may be trying to be too clever for your own good. If you're not happy with your existing company, don't stop applying for jobs elsewhere. Finding the right one may take months; so if you put your search on hold and the rumoured redundancy payments fail to materialize you'll lose valuable time.

But do be picky. Don't take the first thing that comes along. You have the luxury of an income while you look – and if by chance the voluntary redundancy payment does crop up, that'll be a bonus. But, over the long haul, a job that you enjoy in a company with prospects will be worth a great deal more to you than any one-off payment.

Coping with change

Directives have appeared from on high that we must all wear jeans at work on 'Jeans Day' in two months' time, or pay £10 to charity. I don't object to paying money to charity but I do object to the dictatorial way in which this piece of 'fun' is being imposed on everyone. I don't want to wear jeans but nor, on principle, do I want to pay up. I'm not the only one. What should I do?

I agree with the word dictatorial. It does sound an ill-judged bit of management.

But what's not clear from your letter is whether this particular instruction is characteristic of a general management style or an aberration.

If it's the second, be careful not to get too self-righteous about it all. Your phrase 'I'm not the only one' is ominous. It sounds as if groups of you may already be huffing and puffing yourselves into an exaggerated state of indignation. Maybe your boss dictated the note on a busy day after an overnight flight and didn't have time to check it out with anyone. If that's the case, or something like it, find a time to go and see him/her. Don't play the shop steward role; play it light and suggest a draft for another, follow-up memo that would loosen things up without anyone losing face.

The whole thing becomes a great deal more difficult if your

management makes a regular habit of firing off such instructions from the bridge. They've no right to order you to give money to charity – and indeed, these days, are very unwise to 'order' anybody to do anything. The enhancement of authority is seldom achieved by the naked exercise of it.

So if the Jeans Day affair is an all-too-typical example of corporate authoritarianism, you'll need to plan a subtle programme of reform. Talk it through with like-minded people; calmly and soberly. Under no circumstances draft an action plan after four drinks in the winebar on a Friday night.

Check on the structures and procedures that exist within your company. Are there regular sessions where managers listen to the managed? Is there any intranet equivalent to the old suggestions box? If so, use them. Make the helpful point that many of you would like to give more if you were involved more and instructed less. Suggest how it might be done.

Management's first reaction to this well-mannered approach will tell you all you need to know; and whether you should hang on in there or join the escape committee.

My office has recently introduced 'hot-desking' – as many of us work on our clients' sites out of the office, so we don't all need to have a permanent desk. But I hate having to come in to the office and just grab the nearest desk available. I miss having my own desk which I know will always be in the same part of the office, with my own files near it, and with people I know sitting at their desks nearby. I find hot-desking disorientating and waste a lot of time trying to adjust to different surround-

ings. Is there any way I can bring this up without sounding like an outmoded dinosaur?

The picture you paint entrances me. There's this shiny-modern, techno-whirring office full of teenage techno-zealots – happy hot-deskers every one of them. And there's you, huddled at a different workstation every day, a deeply disgruntled and outmoded dinosaur.

I'm not mocking, I promise; I just can't believe that you're as alone as you think you are.

Before your management introduced hot-desking, there was presumably some form of staff consultation. If so, there must have been at least lipservice paid to the need for trial, experiment, feedback – and modification if necessary. This is what you need to pick up on.

But don't do it alone. If you haven't yet exchanged views with some of your colleagues, start now. I'd be astonished if some of them didn't share at least some of your concerns.

Don't allow your pent-up feelings to magnify your discontent: keep it all as cool and thoughtful as you can. Think it all through not just from your point of view but management's as well. Identify and acknowledge any genuine advantages that the changeover has delivered. Then pinpoint the disadvantages and come up with some solutions.

With one or two others (don't make it confrontational), ask for some time with your line manager and offer your joint thoughts for improvement.

This process should lead to some amicable concessions on the part of your company. If not, and if everyone else is as happy as sandboys, then the fanciful picture I started with may not be so fanciful after all. In which case, of course, you'll have to move on.

My company is due to merge with a larger one. Obviously I want to safeguard my job, but I am also concerned about making the right impressions on the new managers who will be entering the company on behalf of our merger partner. Is there any surefire way of doing this without seeming too desperate?

Start by trying to put yourself into the shoes of the new managers. And let's assume they're good people with average levels of common sense and sensitivity.

They'll be acutely aware that mergers and acquisitions induce apprehension. Change is scary enough; being judged by new and unfamiliar masters is even worse. As a result, some people behave in unnatural ways.

The new managers will be on the look-out for this. What they'll be hoping to find will be a bunch of unresentful people simply getting on with their work and being reasonably open-minded when asked to make certain changes to accustomed routines. What they'll be hoping not to find will be either mulish suspicion or gushing sycophancy.

By the sound of it, I don't think you're likely to go for the mulish option; but you might just be tempted to exhibit unnatural enthusiasm for the new order.

Please don't. As you suspect, you'd certainly look desperate.

You'd also repel your new managers and lose every shred of affection that your workmates might feel for you.

Play it cool; play it straight; give it time.

A merger means I have just been made redundant with a generous redundancy package. I am a marketing director and have already had several attractive offers, but I wonder whether I should take the opportunity to start up on my own. On what basis should I make the decision?

There's a significant omission in your question. You talk about starting up on your own but give no indication of what you might actually do. It sounds as if you're entertaining the thought as an abstraction.

Starting a business of your own requires levels of drive and commitment that border on irrationality. Successful entrepreneurs tend to be passionate about something as well as the simple notion of success. They're potty about printing or engineering or catering or computer games or model aeroplanes or old maps or the Internet. That's what gets them through the deeply discouraging early bits; takes them to eight bank managers before they find the right one; enables them to fire an old friend because he's not delivering; keeps them working and worrying seven days a week, often at huge cost to themselves and their families.

You may have all this; but it doesn't sound like it.

It may be you believe that working for yourself is intrinsically more noble than working for others; but that's daft.

You're clearly a good marketing director – which means you've been a success as a member of a team. I sense you wouldn't have even contemplated branching out had it not been for your involuntary redundancy and some unexpected capital. I suspect that you're one of those many people who are by disposition far happier applying a specific skill to an existing enterprise than they would be out there on their own. And there's nothing whatever weedy about that.

With just one caveat, I would urge you strongly to cut the fantasy and take one of your offers.

The caveat is this. If my recommendation fills you with uncontrollable rage, so utterly have I failed to understand your ambitions, then ignore it totally.

I work for a small but high-powered management consultancy. I like my work, the pay is excellent but my hours are ridiculous. I feel I have no life. So I applied for and have been offered a university post, teaching business to graduates. I worry that, if I take the job, I may find teaching isn't for me but, by then, I'll be trapped in a backwater.

You don't tell me your age, nor whether you're bowed down by dependants, mortgages, school fees or other choice-restricting obligations. From what you say, money doesn't seem to be paramount; so on the assumption that you're thirty-five or under and reasonably debt- and fancy-free, my advice would be to take the academic post.

Most people who complain about working ridiculous hours

and having no life never get around to doing anything about it. You have – which suggests you're serious.

And it doesn't, of course, have to be a backwater nor does it have to be for ever. One of the better things about Britain over the last ten years or so has been the disintegration of some of the traditional firewalls between occupations and professions. It's no longer impossible to go from consulting to teaching – and back again if need be. It's also a great deal more acceptable to do two or more things at the same time. So you could start teaching – and keep on a certain amount of private consultancy. Most university business departments actively encourage this sort of work: it keeps you (and them) in touch with what's going on.

As for whether teaching is for you: you'll never know until you try. Think seriously about writing and publishing on your strongest subject: you may never have such long vacations again. And if after three or four years you find the teaching part has become boring and repetitive, get back into business (not necessarily consultancy) – with CV and reputation enhanced. You might also have learnt how to work and live a life at the same time.

Left out of the loop

I am worried my company may collapse. My chief executive is a bit of a dictator and often withholds information. I must find out whether my fears are justified. I have a department to run and my own career to think of. Privately, I think the chief executive's extravagant life-style and lack of judgement are the company's biggest problems.

If you're right in your assessment of your chief executive, he or she will sooner or later bite the dust. The trouble is, it could be too late: so you must do two things.

One, prepare an exit plan for yourself. The chances are, you're going to need a new job – so start the necessary process now. And simultaneously, talk in confidence to your chairman or any non-executive director with whom you have a good relationship.

You cannot in good conscience just tiptoe away, leaving other people and your own department to fend for themselves: you must record your fears with someone. And you must also look after your own future.

But do not, under any circumstances, confuse these two activities – or you will be thought to be politicking. If by happy chance the chief executive gets a swift come-uppance, and your company looks set to prosper again, then you can quietly put your exit plan away in a drawer. But if nothing happens, and your fears persist, then you owe it to yourself and your family to get the hell out.

And remember: the worst that can happen is that you get fired, with hefty compensation, from a company in whose future you have no faith.

I have just joined a design company in a senior client-service capacity. Unfortunately the managerial group has worked together for years and is very tight-knit. I'm not a natural extrovert and I feel like I'm being left out of the loop. How do I make myself heard quickly?

Forget quickly. As a senior account person, you should devote your entire skills and energy towards serving your clients brilliantly. In any creative-service business, anyone who is consistently successful in delivering excellent work is going to be listened to soon enough.

Being part of management seems to have an irresistible draw for a lot of people – not, I think, because the job is intrinsically fascinating: much of it is deeply tedious – but because of the status they think it confers.

Just one caveat. As a client-service director, you'll need to fight from time to time to get the internal resources you need. If you find that your 'tight-knit managerial group' is getting themselves preferential treatment and that you're often at the back of the queue for the creative director, then you must make a move or your clients will suffer. But still don't demand to be 'part of management'. Use client service as your legitimate lever.

Although I am a reasonably successful manager within my company, I've discovered recently that I keep being left out of the loop. Decisions are made without me, and I don't find out about them until several days later than everyone else. The boss also seems to talk much more often with the other managers than with me, and I am never informed what goes on in these discussions either. This never used to be the case, and I know I'm not just being paranoid. Have you got any ideas what might be behind this behaviour, and is there anything I can do about it?

The sentence in your question that intrigues me is, 'This never used to be the case.' So something has changed; and for something to have changed, something else must have happened.

Think hard and self-critically. Did you miss a key strategy meeting? Were you unable to take part in some crucial and competitive presentation? Did you excuse yourself from some important project on the grounds of overwork? Did you decline to step in for a colleague who had problems at home?

I ask because your boss and your colleagues, perhaps not even consciously, seem to have decided that you're not one of the team any more. And it's likely that they came to this conclusion, at least in part, as a result of your own behaviour. I don't think you're being paranoid; but your sense of exclusion may well be self-inflicted.

So be honest with yourself. Have you become more of a loner recently? Have there been changes in your life that have made it harder for you to work late or over weekends?

If this line of thought seems to make sense to you, it may not immediately suggest a solution, but at least you'll feel a little less hurt and bewildered.

You must then decide: have you the time and the inclination to give more of yourself again? Or do you now, entirely reasonably, believe that there's more to life than total work immersion?

If you feel the former, demonstrate it; and your boss and your colleagues will very soon notice. If you feel the latter, you should probably be thinking of another kind of job altogether.

How do I know when it's time to move on?

I am a senior lawyer, who enjoys working on big cases and have done well at that. Over the past twelve years I have been given more responsibility and exciting work. The senior partner now tells me unless I do more selling of the company I am unlikely to be made a partner. I don't like selling and I don't want to be a manager or a bureaucrat, but I want to be a partner. Should I leave the practice?

There are two possibilities here. Either your senior partner's an idiot or you haven't heard what he's really saying.

If you're as good as you say at what you do, and as bad as you say at selling (whatever that might mean), he's insane to want you to change your way of working.

But what he might be saying is that partners aren't called partners for nothing. They're not supposed to be selfish; they're supposed to be all in it together (the big consultancies are very hot on this) – but that's not how you seem to work. In other words, he may be trying to tell you that until you show you can join in and help others and do a bit of work for the common good, then you haven't demonstrated the right partnership qualities.

Only you will know which of these possibilities is the right one.

If he's an idiot, get out. But if he's just giving you a nudge or two, then mend your ways, stay on – and prosper.

I am a departmental head of an international business, which lacks IT representation at board level. The result is that I spend my whole time chasing processes instead of doing the creative thinking I was brought in for. The board directors make assurances but fail to deliver. Am I on a hiding to nothing?

Were I a sceptical person, I'd interpret your question in an unsympathetic light. Most departmental job descriptions, however honeyed the terminology, demand some element of day-to-day administration (or process-chasing) as well as 'creative thinking'. Were I a sceptical person, I'd suspect you of hoping to dodge all the dreary bits on the debatable grounds that they prevent your imagination soaring into a stratosphere of unfettered speculation. So my first piece of advice is that you should examine yourself and your motives with clinical objectivity. Nobody can be a 'creative thinker' on a 24/7 basis. A bit of process-chasing and mixing with the masses helps feet stay on the ground – and may even stimulate you in your more inventive moments. Are you absolutely certain that it's not time you're short of but good ideas?

However, you probably find this suggestion both offensive and without foundation; in which case, you must trace the steps that led you here.

You talk about 'board directors' in the plural – but there's presumably a specific director to whom you report? (Somebody must have hired you.) Book some time – and go over with them the reasons why you were taken on. Suggest that there must be disappointment that so little constructive creative thinking has yet come through. Explain that you share this disappointment. Identify any examples you can of superior performance by competitors. Point out that, not only are you failing to do what you're paid for, but the company as a whole is already losing ground and will certainly lose more if things don't change. Suggest those changes.

The changes you ask for should be specific and workable. Add a time-scale: ask for another formal review on a given future date, and agree the date there and then: you'll know what's realistic.

If none of this works, then you'll know that you are indeed on a hiding to nothing and can put in a call to your favourite headhunter. But if the changes are made and the deadline agreed, then you'll have every chance to prove your point.

My business partner and I started our business several years ago. We're now in our fifties and the business is doing well. Recently, my partner's son joined us, and he has gradually taken over much of my work – leaving me the menial tasks. When I confronted my business partner, he said he and his son wanted to buy me out of the business. I am devastated – I thought he was a good friend and that we'd continue running the business together for years. I don't want to leave the business, but feel outnumbered by my partner and his son.

I'm afraid this answer may infuriate you, but my only alternative would be such pussy-footing tactfulness that I'd probably fail to get the point across altogether.

You need, I'm pretty sure, to begin to prepare yourself for an ordered withdrawal from your business. You may think this unfair – and it probably is – but the evidence suggests that your relationship with your partner has been less than open for some time and I seriously doubt if it can now be repaired. For example: when it was first suggested that his son should join the company, you obviously didn't talk through the implications. That was the time, without heat or suspicion, to have discussed the future of your company and its management – but that chance has now gone, and I fear for ever. (I warned you I was going to be infuriating.)

You're perfectly free, of course, to reject his offer; but if you do, this is what you inevitably face: deeply uncomfortable working relationships with both your partner and his son; more and more menial and unrewarding tasks; and a corrosive sense of resentment that will make you an increasingly unlikeable person – even to yourself. It's a bleak and undignified prospect and I hope you decide to exchange it for another.

Draw a line under your devastation. Practise being heroically dispassionate. Recognize that, since both you and your partner are in your fifties, it's not too soon to be planning management succession.

Insist on an independent valuation of your company. Don't flounce; take your time; be sure you get a fair price. Meanwhile, start planning the second half of your life: you should have quite enough capital to embark on another business adventure as well as securing yourself a fret-free retirement.

My direct contemporary is flooded with good projects, while I seem to get the dregs and can rarely keep myself busy beyond 5.30. My director says he's happy with my 'progress'. I have asked for more to do but, three months later, no further work has materialized. Am I being discreetly pushed out?

I don't know if you're being pushed out, exactly: but somebody's sending you a message, all right – even if they don't realize it.

Take a deep breath, employ a mighty effort of will – and try to look at the situation not through your own eyes but through those of your director.

What does he see? He sees two people: one of whom he keeps very busy and one of whom has little to do by 5.30. Why should that be? What's the difference between them? And I don't want *your* opinion here: I want your best guess at your director's opinion. How does he see you both?

Does he find you boring? Does he find you able but plodding? Does he find your competitive contemporary quicker-witted and more fun? And I'm not getting at you here: you don't have to agree with your director's view, just understand it.

Because it's obviously not ideal for him, is it? He's got one overworked and one underworked junior when he'd much rather be able to push projects at both with equal confidence.

If basic ability was the problem, I doubt if you'd still be there.

So think hard about style and manner – and see if the workload begins to pick up. If it doesn't, look around.

I moved to my current job because I was told that there would be opportunities to travel overseas and use my languages. There are – but my boss always seems to nab them, leaving me to do the donkey work at home. Is it worth sitting it out? I have tentatively raised the subject with my boss, who appears sympathetic but fails to deliver.

A lot of life's knottier problems have one thing in common: they creep up on us, very gradually, bit by bit; and there's rarely an obvious, clear-cut moment that prompts us to say, 'Right! Enough of this! Things have got to change around here!' So we give things another chance, mutter, 'Next time I'll really give them a piece of my mind . . .' – and of course drift and discontent continue.

When faced with one of these insidious, creeping predicaments, the best thing to do is to decide, well ahead of time, on a clear, measurable trigger moment for yourself. Write it down; and then (unless something happens to change the game) stick to it. In your case it should probably be the number of months that have passed since you joined with still no overseas trip to show for it. But it's got to be a number – not some ill-defined feeling of frustration.

When that number comes up, send a note to your boss. I know it sounds formal, but you need to be in writing and you need to be precise. Keep heat out of it. Don't sound huffy. Just say that an important contributory reason for your taking the job was the opportunity it promised for travel. Now, x months later, your languages, an important part of your qualifications, are growing rusty. You can't afford to let your market value diminish any further; so, with regret, you'll soon need to move on.

Last tip. Write the note now. Then read it back to yourself and see how it sounds. It'll help you discover just how important travel really is for you – and whether you really would ditch your current job in order to get some. If you wouldn't, stop whingeing and get on with it.

My uncle is chairman of the business I run as MD. It is profitable but he is holding it back. Everything I do is overturned by him. How can I get rid of him? Each of our families owns 50 per cent of the business.

Now you know why so many experts warn against 50/50 owner-ship. It so often leads to tears – or even worse, to stultification. That's what seems to be happening to you.

So don't struggle on, getting more and more resentful. Go for clarification.

Tell your board (I hope you've got one) that the company is suffering from blurred lines of responsibility and that you have two recommendations to make.

First, that the chairman's role be confirmed as non-executive and that you, as managing director, are clearly the chief execu-tive; and second, to reflect this distinction, your uncle's family should sell, say, 5 per cent of their shares to your family – thereby making ownership 55/45 in your favour.

I don't know the politics and I don't know the composition of your board – but at least this will bring matters to a head. If your recommendations are accepted, you may have a sulky uncle on your hands but he won't be able (at least as easily) to undermine your authority. And if your recommendations are rejected, then you'll know it's time for you to move on.

Running a family business can get very fraught and claustro-phobic as you've already discovered. But there is a world else-where. If you're any good, this could be an important opportunity for you.

The owner gave staff an 'all pull together' speech only four months ago. The workforce are extremely loyal, have put in long hours and make little fuss. So, as MD, I was horrified to discover that he has ordered a new Jaguar XKR on the company. He argues it's important to maintain company image. This will create waves. How can I get him to back down without losing face?

A couple of interesting points here. The man's an 'owner' – and it sounds as if he's the sole and outright owner. And the fact that you 'discovered' that he'd ordered his ostentatious car suggests that he treats the business as his private fiefdom. If so, this must make it quite difficult for you, as a salaried MD, to establish your own authority. So I suspect the car affair is not an isolated incident but part of a general pattern.

If this is an accurate analysis, then you might as well look upon the Jaguar issue not as a challenge but more an opportunity to get a whole lot of stuff out into the open. I bet you don't find this a particularly enticing prospect but you'll have to do it some time, so why not now?

Start by being quite clear on one thing. In any fight to the death between the outright owner of a private company and his salaried MD, there can be only one winner. Forget about justice, common sense, gratitude and what's best for the business. If he wants to have his way, he will. So you must go into this exchange recognizing that, at the end of it, you may have to leave. Whatever you do, don't start off pretending to be resolute only to subject yourself later to a series of shaming concessions.

Have a grown-up conversation. Make it clear that he's quite entitled to have his Jaguar on the firm but that's not the principle at issue. The principle is whether he needs a good MD or not. A good MD must command the respect of his workforce – which the best of men will fail to achieve if undermined by the owner. So why pay a good salary to someone who you then render ineffective?

You are in absolutely no doubt: it will greatly benefit his company if he forgets about the XKR. If he ignores this advice, then it's clear to you, without heat or petulance, that he believes he doesn't need you.

Good luck. My guess is that you'll be well out of it.

I went on a gruelling annual work conference and used the spa facilities at the hotel (on the recommendation of my col-

leagues). When I tried to reclaim the cost as expenses, my CEO refused my claim. He says he paid his own spa costs this time last year but I have checked the records and know this is not the case.

This is all very interesting. I don't think you're telling me that you've had a claim for fifty quids' worth of expenses turned down. I think you're telling me that you and your CEO are not on the best of terms, that you haven't trusted him for some time and that you've now unearthed evidence that you're right not to trust him. Why else would you have taken the trouble (and run the risk) of checking his year-old expenses?

What I also infer is that the unease you feel about each other is a form of competitiveness: why else, unless he's a congenital fibber, should he lie to you? I think he knows you're a bit iffy about him and wasn't going to give you the pleasure of being in the right. Not very grown-up, I agree: but human enough.

All of this is both extremely petty and extremely serious. This is how marriages come to an end. This is why Henry storms out of the house forever because Prue never puts the top back on the toothpaste tube: the most trivial of misdemeanours being asked to bear the full responsibility for years of accumulated doubt and discontentment.

This sort of relationship can be repaired – but it takes low cunning and a painful smidgen of selflessness.

If there's going to be an easing of tension, you probably feel that it's up to your CEO to make the first move. After all, he's the top banana. What's more, you're in the right and he's not.

Absolutely correct; but forget all that stuff. Be mature beyond your years. He may not deserve it – but try and make it easy for him. Take him out to lunch (not, I suggest, on expenses) and ask him what else you can do to be of use to the company.

If he doesn't respond – or if you have very good reason to believe that he's chronically untrustworthy – start preparing yourself for a career change. He doesn't deserve you.

I am beginning to realize that my recent job move has been a bad one. But, if I try to cut my losses by applying elsewhere, my CV may look 'butterfly' to other potential employers, because I was headhunted from my previous job within six months. My old job has been filled. What should I do?

I wonder why you left your previous job after only six months? Simply to say you were headhunted suggests you have no will of your own. You must have liked the job well enough – you imply you'd go back if the job was still open – so what went on? Was it just money? Or vanity? Were you competing with someone? Or did you think that all promotion was good promotion?

Before you make your next decision, sort out the reasons for your last one – as honestly as you can. It won't stop you making another mistake – but it might just stop you making the same one again.

Next: how certain are you that your new job really is a disaster? If you were headhunted, you were probably subjected to a comprehensive snowjob. So it's entirely possible that if you weren't still making unfavourable comparisons between the job as you found it and its romanticized prospectus, you'd be perfectly happy: at least for long enough to escape any butterfly accusations.

But if, after all this, you're still convinced the job is not for you, then the sooner you pack up your pencil-box the better; as long as you march off in the right direction. And that, of course, presents you with a problem – because it might take as much as a year to find what you want. So I suggest that your first action should be to register your interest in moving with a headhunter (though not, obviously, the one who got you into all this). They may or may not deliver the goods – but the real value of this move is that it allows you to demonstrate in future interviews that you did recognize your mistake immediately.

I'll resist the temptation to say that you'd better get it right this time. I expect you've thought of that yourself.

I was delighted recently to be offered a senior position with a well-known, family-run manufacturer. On joining, however, I realize it has dire problems that weren't apparent from the outside – financial insecurity, an unhappy workforce and an indecisive board. I could see this as a challenge but my instinct is to cut and run. What do you think?

I don't want to sound unsympathetic – but why in the name of Stephen Byers did you join this shambles in the first place?

You say your new company has 'dire problems that weren't apparent in the first place'. It's no good blaming problems for not being apparent. Problems go to great lengths not to be apparent. You've got to blame yourself for not rootling them out. And by the sound of it, they wouldn't have taken much rootling.

The fact that it's family run should have triggered the first alarm-bell. Family-run firms have two classes of citizen: family – and the rest. It's not villainy: it's just that people who own companies identify with them so closely that they simply can't distinguish between personal things and business things. And if you're not family, then you're hired help.

A lot of people seem to go all soft in the head when they're offered a job. Golly-gosh – somebody wants me to be a director! How sweet of them! You don't have to become a bitter old cynic to make room for a little healthy scepticism. Just ask a few beady questions. Why do they need you? What happened to your predecessors? Can you talk to them? Can you talk to the company's auditors? Who do you know in the workforce? Find out which pub people go to after work for a pint and a grumble, then go there yourself and hang around a bit.

I'm only telling you all this because next time you'd better be a great deal more careful. And by the sound of it, next time can't come too soon. Yes, certainly: you should cut and run. But do please work out first where you're going to run to.

After spending ten years with the same retail company, I have finally moved on for all the usual reasons – better prospects elsewhere, higher salary, new challenges and so on. To my surprise, I'm still finding it hard to settle into my new job after nine months, and I miss my old one. I'm thirty-nine and single, and my social life was built around my former colleagues. My old company has since offered me my job back – although this time with slightly more responsibility and better pay. I've always thought that it was a bad move to go back to something, but in this case I'm really tempted to return.

Reluctance to return to an old job is often based on little more than embarrassment. Your old company gave you a rattling good leaving party, a better present than you had any right to expect and the boss man stood up and said some extremely generous things about you. You in turn were grateful and gracious – but left them in no doubt that you were leaving for all the things you tell me you were leaving for: better prospects, higher salary, new challenges.

And now, lurking somewhere in the back of your head, is the prospect of a slightly sheepish return. Turning up on that first morning won't be easy. Jokes will be made at your expense, not all of them affectionate. Even with the promise of more responsibility and better pay, it's still going to seem a bit of a climbdown, a bit of a humiliation.

Which it is, in a way, but – except in your own mind and perhaps that of your worst enemy – this is a very small failure indeed: a legitimate experiment that didn't come off; but valuable lessons learned.

The great thing is that your old company wants you back. Management will be doubly delighted: they'll be pleased to welcome a face they trust and your return may make other potential defectors think twice. And most of your workmates – who you obviously get along with – will be reassured to learn that the grass isn't all that greener after all.

I can think of only one reason for further hesitation. Once you're back, you'll be back – not necessarily for good, but for a very long time. If that doesn't daunt you, then swallow the pride, be extremely grateful to your existing employers – and head off home.

I've been the deputy director of a small retail chain for fifteen years. I was always widely tipped to be the director of the company, and have been happy to wait. But at fifty-five, the director shows no signs of wanting to retire for another ten years, and, frankly, I'm not getting any younger. To complicate matters further, there have been a few hints that our director might also be considering the finance director as his successor. At forty-five, should I just cut my losses and leave?

You probably don't see your boss as Winston Churchill but I'm pretty certain that fate has cast you as Anthony Eden. Fifteen years is a very long time to be a deputy anything. In another ten years, you'll have been director-in-waiting for most of your working life. By the time that Eden finally got the job, he was well past doing it; and, harsh though it sounds, the same will inevitably be true for you.

The appointment of a new director, particularly after twenty years or more, should usually be a trigger for change; for the introduction of new ideas and new energy. Everyone on the payroll should feel a sort of tingle: revived expectations with maybe an invigorating touch of apprehension. It's everyone-on-their-toes time again. Through no fault of your own, it's just not possible that as familiar and comfortable a figure as you would be able to generate such a sense of excitement.

The fact that you've been content to wait on the touchline for as long as you have suggests that you aren't obsessively ambitious. But you must have certain skills and enthusiasms. So put your present company behind you and wallow in fantasy for a bit. What's your absolutely top dream job – one that would send you whistling off to work of a Monday morning? Identify that; then go for it. The sooner you start, the better your chances.

I've had a relatively senior role in a large retail organization for the past two years. I get on well with my colleagues and my appraisals have been positive. The problem is that I have been here on a series of short-term six-month contracts. I've spoken to my immediate boss about achieving a more permanent footing, but he says there is nothing he can do. In the meantime I am not eligible for the company pension scheme, I don't take holidays in case it's used as a reason for not renewing my contract, and I feel very insecure about my future. Is there anything I can do to change the situation?

I can see that this is very unsatisfactory – and a bit suspicious, too. As a large organization, your company is bound to have a personnel (I expect they call it HR) department. Now's the time to short-circuit your immediate boss and go straight to them. They're the people who know more about contracts and company policies than any line manager.

Ask them to tell you just why you've been kept on a series

of six-month contracts with all the attendant disadvantages. Remind them of your positive appraisals. Tell them of your reluctance to take holidays (which I have to say I find rather weedy of you).

As you'll certainly recognize, this approach carries risks. One possible explanation for your company's behaviour is that they're unconvinced of your long-term value but haven't yet got around to saying so. By bringing the issue to a head, you may well be precipitating your own departure. But by the sound of it, that might be no bad thing.

I am a Business Studies graduate and have completed nearly one year of a two-year Graduate Training Scheme with a large company. There is a chance that I may sometime soon be offered a permanent role within this company. Do you suggest that I should complete my final year's training and gain more experience by doing so, or should I start in a permanent and more specialized role with this company as soon as one becomes available?

This is a more difficult decision now than it would have been only a few years ago. A few years ago I would have found it easy enough to make sonorous parental noises: reminding you of your obligations, firmly advising you to stay the full course of your training scheme, pointing out that you might never again be offered an opportunity to gain general experience – and painting in lurid colours the long-term risks of premature specialization.

Today, however, it's not so obvious. If your specialized role is part of the e-revolution (which sounds likely), it just might be too good an offer to refuse. Things move so quickly that a year's experience in that sort of job can be equivalent to five or more years in the old way of doing things.

So check it through carefully. If you believe there's a reasonable chance of another permanent job, at least as interesting, being open to you at the end of your two full years – then curb your impatience, stay the course and complete your training. For all the boringly responsible reasons given above, you won't regret it. But if you have a very strong instinct that the specialized opportunity open to you now might just be one of those never-to-be-repeated, fast-lane affairs, then cross your fingers and go for it.

And if you're really wise, you'll use any spare time you might have trying to pick up the wider experience you elected to forgo.

6 | *Is honesty always the right policy?*

Every now and then it emerges that some highly successful business-man has been less than totally truthful in compiling his entry to Who's Who? That business degree from Harvard, it seems, was really more of a six-week course; and why does his three-year stint with Robert Maxwell earn no mention at all? The ridicule released by the exposure of these petty deceits invariably outweighs any small benefit they might have conferred; yet the instinct to conceal or embroider continues.

Which is odd; because the business world is a good deal more open and a good deal less intolerant than it was even twenty years ago. Twenty years ago important executives were expected to be white male heterosexuals from good schools and with good tailors. Today, sexual orientation is only rarely an issue; women chief executives, though still the exception, are no longer the butt of locker-room jokes; your place of education is largely irrelevant; and you can often wear what you want.

The problem usually starts at some early and critical point in a person's working life. It's been hard to get a job; three consecutive interviews have yielded nothing; money's running out. It seems a minor thing, then, to conceal a little something or add gloss to a qualification. Nothing particularly shameful, of course: but, who knows, it might just tip the balance.

The trouble is, it's there for ever, like a time-capsule, waiting to be rediscovered. With very few exceptions, it's far, far better to play it straight.

One of the senior partners at my law firm has asked me to a weekend lunch party at his house. He suggested I bring my other half – the problem is that he is clearly expecting (and would prefer) me to bring a girlfriend and I am gay. Do I pretend that I have no partner, bring a female friend or take my male partner?

I just hope you haven't led him to believe that you're straight. If so, you're in a smallish pickle of your own making. If not, this could be the perfect opportunity for you to sort things out once and for all.

The key is the lunch party. Lunch parties like this one tend to have table seating plans. So say to your senior partner, 'I'm very grateful to you and your wife for the invitation. As it happens, my other half is a man – and I can quite see that this might throw out your seating plan. Why don't you talk it over with your wife? For my part, I'd be equally happy to come with my partner, come with a girl friend, come on my own – or not come at all. Do please let me know which would suit you best.' Exact words are important here – so you might find it easier to do it in a handwritten note. It also gives the senior partner and his wife a little longer to adjust their facial expressions and their prejudices.

If their response suggests that your homosexuality is likely to prove a serious handicap to you in your career, then you should move to a more enlightened firm as soon as possible. Nobody should have to live a lie.

I have recently started taking Prozac. Should I tell my boss? I have a good track record at work and have recently received glowing appraisals.

Did you discuss this with your doctor? If not, do so next time you renew your prescription. Most doctors will say it's up to you – and so it should be. But it's always better to ask, just in case there's some special circumstance.

So if that's the advice you're given, do you spill the beans? To me, the beans are so absurdly insignificant that I can see no point whatsoever in spilling them.

Would you confess to your boss that were taking Zantac? Or Vitamin C? Or Californian Syrup of Figs? He'd give you a decidedly old-fashioned look if you did.

There's still this lingering, medieval superstition around that minor disorders of the head are somehow more sinister and more shameful than minor disorders of the body. You seem to believe in it.

Millions take Prozac – and feel better for it. If you, too, benefit from it, then so will your work. Your glowing appraisals suggest that it already is.

I can think of only one possible circumstance in which disclosure could be advisable. If there's any specific task you continue to find particularly stressful, then you might be wise to mention it. As long as it's not absolutely central to your job, most good bosses will understand and be happy to accommodate you.

Five years ago I had an office affair with a junior member of staff. We were both unattached, but it ended very badly and she left the company, claiming that I had hindered her chances for promotion. She never launched a formal complaint, but I know from mutual friends that she remains very bitter. I have since moved on, but have just found out that she is joining my new company in a role close to mine. She did not, and probably still doesn't know, that I work here, and my new colleagues don't know that I know her. I'm worried that she might make my life here very difficult, and wonder whether I should warn my managers of our previous relationship.

Wow, what a nightmare. I've done a fairly thorough trawl through your shortlist of options and I can't pretend that any of them beckons very temptingly; but at least we can probably eliminate a couple.

Warning your managers has a superficial attraction in that it gets things out in the open right away. But I wonder if it appeals to you for a less respectable reason: the opportunity to get your version of the story in first? And what exactly would you tell them? And what would you expect them to do with the information once they had it? You can hardly expect them to cancel her job offer. I suppose they might just try to find a role for her in a different part of the company – but even that would compromise them a little. No: that option's out, at least for the moment. You'll only embarrass your managers – and they won't thank you for that.

Next in line is to do nothing: always an attractive option and surprisingly often right. But the risk here is considerable. It's true that if she's changed and settled down and even formed a new attachment, it could well be that all your apprehensions turn out to be unfounded. But that's not what your mutual friends are telling you so you'd be unwise to bank on it. No, I'm afraid you've got to do something – and I'd start with those mutual friends of yours.

I find it odd that they've told you about her imminent job-move but apparently haven't told her that you're already there. If they really are friends, they won't want her turning up for work on her first morning, all shiny-eyed and bushy-tailed – only to be brought up short by the sight of your baleful countenance at the next work station.

So first, ask the mutual friends to come clean and tell her the score. And secondly, ask them, on your behalf, to suggest a meeting just between the two of you. It's almost certainly the last suggestion in the world you want to hear but I'm afraid you'd better do it. How she responds will tell you all you need to know – and what, if anything, you need to do next.

(Why, I wonder, am I left with the unworthy suspicion that you really did behave badly towards her, all those years ago?)

I am looking for my first job after completing a university degree, but my problem is that I suffer from dyslexia. It affects my reading and writing quite severely, but as I am looking for a job in stockbroking I'm hoping that it won't be too much of an issue. My concern is whether I should tell interviewers that I suffer from dyslexia or whether this would be likely to count against me when I'm trying to find a job?

This is an important decision, because the two choices open to you carry quite different sorts of risk.

As you rightly suspect, if you do come clean about your dyslexia it could well count against you in interviews; but at least you've come clean. If you conceal your disability, and get a job, you'll have nagging anxieties just about for ever: first, that you got a job under false pretences; and second that at some future point, sooner or later, never mind how – the truth will out.

So I'd go for openness and do it boldly. Reveal your dyslexia up front, acknowledge that it's entirely reasonable for any prospective employer to be concerned about its potential effect on your work and explain how you've overcome the problem so far. You have, after all, obtained your degree – which must, presumably, have required some proficiency in reading and writing.

You've probably had contact with the International Dyslexia Association already, so double check with them about this approach and see if they have examples in the public domain of well-known people who have been highly successful despite their dyslexia. Employers find precedents reassuring. If all else fails, you can always resort to subterfuge. But I hope and believe you won't have to.

I was dismissed for disorderly conduct fifteen years ago and have been self-employed since. Does the dismissal still count against me if I want to look for a new job? I'm a reformed character since those days, and don't want to bring the matter up unless I have to.

Being dismissed for disorderly conduct isn't the same as having a criminal record. It probably weighs more heavily with you than it would with a prospective employer. My instinct, therefore, is that you should go for total openness and transparency.

You should always assume, however improbable it may seem, that your distant dismissal will become known. Some mischievous god is bound to ensure that the office cleaner who long ago found you drunk and disorderly in the computer room is now the lovely old biddy in your new staff canteen.

Put yourself in the place of any potential employer. Which would cause you the greater concern: open admission of an ancient indiscretion; or unearthed evidence of current deceit?

If you do decide to come clean, and I hope you do, make sure you're well equipped with references. Since you've been self-employed, they obviously can't be from employers. But long-standing, satisfied customers can be just as reassuring; and maybe a letter from your GP. Just be dead straight about it: 'Why should you believe me when I say I've been a reformed character for the last fifteen years? So here's some supporting evidence – and do please feel free to call them.'

I was fired from my senior sales job three weeks ago, and I still haven't told my family. I pretend to go to work every day and instead spend the day at the local library applying for jobs. I feel terrible about deceiving my wife and our two young children, but I can't bring myself to tell them. And I might be offered a job in the next week or so – then they won't ever need to know and I won't have worried them. What should I do?

My first instinct was to feel huge sympathy for you. You're not, of course, the first to find himself in this appalling predicament – but that's small comfort.

When I'd thought about you for a little longer, however, I began to feel a certain impatience. Just why is it, I began to wonder, that you can't bring yourself to tell your wife and family? You suggest it's because you don't want to worry them, but I'm not so sure. You don't tell me why you were fired – but unless it was for something truly shameful, why do you seem to feel ashamed?

You've got to be fierce with yourself about this – and it won't be easy. But you must remind yourself that the loss of a job, however traumatic, is no good reason for discarding all self-respect. Your job was an important part of you – but only a part. Your wife and children and friends don't define you only by what you do. You haven't lost your character, your spirit, your intelligence. You haven't lost whatever it is that makes your family rate you.

So however embarrassing it may seem, you must extricate yourself from this daily deceit immediately. You must tell your wife everything. Don't pretend that you've only just been sacked: tell her absolutely everything, including why you haven't told her before. The longer you leave it, the more difficult it will become.

I'll be astonished if she thinks the less of you for all this. And the lifting of the burden of deception, and the addition of her support, will give you a lot of added confidence as you go about finding that new job.

Should you also tell your children? Discuss that with your wife – her instinct is likely to be sounder than yours. My own hunch is that you should come clean about the job loss but not about when it happened: a legitimate compromise, I think.

7 | *Which comes first: firm or family?*

It's always unwise to make comparisons across time – but most workplace problems have probably eased a little over the last twenty years or so. This one has undoubtedly intensified.

It was never completely like this – and I'm certainly not advocating that it ever should be again – but this is how once it seemed to be.

The husband had a job and the wife didn't. He left the house every morning and came back when the children were already in bed. She stayed at home, cooked, cleaned, shopped, did the washing and looked after the children. If work kept him late, or took him away, it was quite understood. And there were always the weekends and holidays, when they could all be together.

Of course, even then, there were tensions. Competition for time has always existed. There can be few working parents, of either sex, or of any time, who've never felt a pang of guilt.

But today it's harder still. More women have jobs. More men do more about the house: sometimes even do their share of bathtime. Mothers, too, have to work late and travel.

And all the time, companies have been getting increasingly competitive, expecting more commitment, more single-minded concentration on the next new business opportunity.

It's got a lot more difficult all round; but I don't have the slightest doubt that the tug-of-war between work and home causes a great deal more anguish to working mothers than to working fathers.

Biology, and the memory of how it was, both favour men.

At my company there is a strong culture, led from the very top, of drinking at lunchtime and after work. Alcohol at lunchtime wipes me out, and after work I want to go home to my family. But I'm a senior manager and I don't want to appear stand-offish and damage my chances of promotion. What should I do?

However difficult it may seem, what you should do is what your instinct tells you to do.

If alcohol at lunchtime wipes you out, skip it. Tell anybody who's interested that alcohol at lunchtime wipes you out.

If you like to get back to your family after work, do so: if only because the alternatives are too grisly to contemplate. You either stand there in the pub, clutching half a lager and laughing unconvincingly at other people's rude jokes; or you quite unconsciously transmit such strong signals of superiority and disapproval that you won't even get brownie points for having joined in.

Nothing is more obvious, nor more dispiriting for others,

than someone who is not naturally one of the lads pretending, with limited acting ability, to be one.

You will already have spotted the snag. The culture you describe is 'led from the very top'. From this it is clear that your big boss, who is possibly even the owner, continues to need the company and security of a loyal group of courtiers – or syco-phants as you may more accurately think them to be.

So if it is really true, and not just a product of your troubled imagination, that the ability to stay late drinking with the boys is a non-negotiable qualification for promotion, then start read-ing the classifieds. But talk to the big banana first. If you're good at what you do, and you seem to be, my guess is that a clear understanding between you and the boss will suit both of you. You continue to be a valued senior manager for him; and he makes no unreasonable demands on your own social time.

You will, of course, have to learn to take the inevitable boring badinage in good spirit – or at least pretend to. But that's a small price to pay for seeing the kids into bed every night.

I have a part-time job as clerk in a law firm and leave at 3 p.m. every day to go home to my children. Recently my office has started holding a weekly 'team meeting' at 4 p.m., which I am expected to attend. They say they can't change the time, but I'm not being paid overtime for the additional hours I spend in the office, and I end up paying extra for the childminder at home. What can I do if it's just my preference against all of theirs?

On the face of it, this does sound wrong – and I can quite understand your sense of injustice. But let me probe a little deeper.

Am I right in thinking that the 4 p.m. 'team meeting' is an idea dreamt up by the team itself rather than by management? If so, this does suggest to me that relationships between you all aren't as good as they should be. A team that really felt itself a team wouldn't be so thoughtless as to put one of its members to such expensive inconvenience.

Since you seem to be the only part-timer, or at least the only member who leaves work at 3, I wonder if this could be at the root of it all. I know it shouldn't happen – but the closer and more competitive a team, the more they will resent any apparent lack of commitment. You know it's not that; but teams are funny things. And if all the others have a beer or two after their meeting, and you're the only one not there, the sense of distance between them and you can only widen.

If this analysis makes sense to you; and you've already tried and failed to get the time of the meeting changed; and your line manager declines to recommend you for overtime: then I think you should steel yourself for a change of job. Flexible working hours have much to be said for them – but they can play havoc with group morale.

I feel guilty when I leave work on time but miss seeing my two young children if I don't. Lately, my boss has started to 'joke' about part-timers – even though I usually start well before him – and I am worried that he thinks I am not dedicated enough.

Conscientious people are famously good at feeling guilty. It's the lazy ones who whistle their carefree way through life. So you must try to sort out in your own mind whether your guilt is justified or not.

If you put in the hours and never leave important work unfinished, your conscience should be absolutely clear. So perhaps you feel guilty because you don't go for a beer with the boys after work?

You're clearly very sensitive on this issue – that's OK: most thoughtful people are – but this could easily mean that you're reading far more into your boss's 'jokes' than he intends. (From the sound of it, sensitivity isn't his own most striking characteristic.)

If the jokes continue and you go on fretting, pick a good time to have a word with him. Don't make a big thing of it, don't refer to the jokes and don't say you feel guilty. Just say how much you value seeing your children in the evening and ask him to tip you off at once if he thinks it's making you in any way less effective. Whatever his response, it's bound to be enlightening.

And if all goes well, it might even put a bit of a damper on the jokes.

I have been offered a three-year posting to head my company's South American operations. But I must consider my children's schooling, the fact that none of my family speaks Spanish and that we shall need a bodyguard at all times. How do I explain to the satisfaction of my employers that I am dedicated to the company but cannot ignore my family's needs?

Every instinct tells me that you don't really want to do it anyway. I'm sure your concerns for family are genuine enough – but you show none of the normal signs of being torn between your own personal excitement at the prospect of the job and your family's well-being. So if you secretly don't much want it (for whatever reason) and you also have serious doubts about its consequences for your family, then at least the decision is an easy one – even if conveying it to your company is not.

What I suggest you say is something like this: 'The job's a big one and I'm thrilled to have been offered it. To do it well, I'd need to be totally confident and totally committed. Because of my family, I don't think I could be – and that would be unfair on the company. I'm sure you understand.'

But just before you say that: are you sure you're making the right decision? Three years is not a lifetime. Do you know what your family really feels – or are you making assumptions? You must have friends or colleagues out there already: have you spoken to them? Of course it would be strange and challenging – and there would certainly be many hairy moments. But it could be a hugely stimulating and formative three years for all of you.

I booked a holiday to attend my best friend's wedding in America, giving my boss months of notice. With one week to go, he scheduled a meeting, which he said was crucial and I had to attend. Although he paid to fly me out later, I missed the wedding and only briefly saw my friends before they went on honeymoon. How do I tell my boss his behaviour was out of line?

The part of your question I find most interesting is when you ask, 'How do I tell my boss his behaviour was out of line?' You assume without question that it was – and of course it may have been. But surely it all depends on the nature of that particular crucial meeting?

One of the most common complaints from people in business is lack of involvement. They feel there's always some corporate layer, just one tantalizing rung above them, where all the interesting things are decided and where individual contributions can have a decisive effect. They long to be indispensable and to bask in greater public recognition.

So if you're lucky enough to have such a job, then you must also expect some degree of pain: not least, a constant tug-of-war between personal time and professional time.

The more valued you are, and the more conscientious you are, the more such conflicts will arise. But whatever you do, don't try to generalize: take them one-by-one. It will always be difficult, but there will certainly be times when you should want to put a crucial meeting (assuming it really is crucial) before a best friend's wedding. And which went into the diary first is totally irrelevant.

So was that meeting really crucial? Was your presence clearly important? Or was your boss just playing silly-buggers? If the former, shut up and count your blessings: you've got a job that thousands of others would die for – *and* a free trip to America.

If the latter, look for a new boss.

I recently moved out of London, where I work, and my daily commute has become overlong and tiring. My job is specialist with few good opportunities outside the city. I don't really need to be in the office every day but my boss, perhaps understandably, doesn't want to create a precedent. I feel torn. I want my job but seem to be constantly exhausted.

You don't say what prompted you to move out of London in the first place. You must have known that commuting can be a pain so I have to assume that there were compensating attractions; or at least you thought there would be. Bigger, cheaper accommodation, perhaps? Or better schools? Or weekends away from town and traffic? If one or more of the above, the first thing you must calculate is how much of what you hoped for you got and how much you value it.

And not just you. It's odd you make no mention of your family. You use the word 'I' five times and the word 'my' four times and present the problem as a purely personal one – so either you haven't got a family (which somehow I doubt) or you're being very slightly egocentric about all this.

So: if you (and/or your possibly non-existent family) have gained quite a lot from your move then you should decide to stay where you are and work out the best way of reducing the hassle and the exhaustion. You say you've moved only recently. Unfamiliar routines are invariably more tiring than familiar ones – so simply giving yourself a little more time may in itself be helpful.

Then try a little harder with your boss. Tell him you're sure you could be more productive with a different work pattern.

Suggest a trial period, during which you work, say, two days a week from home and three from the office. Ask him to appoint a 'jury' – two colleagues, for example, two clients and himself – who will be asked to pass judgement at the end of the experiment on whether your work has suffered or not. And promise him that, whatever the verdict, you'll happily accept it.

At the very least, you'll have a better basis for future decision-making; and it might even work a storm.

My husband and I run our own company. Do you have any ideas on how to maintain 'Chinese walls' between work and home?

I'm not sure why you want to. Is it that you're dealing with confidential client matters? Is it that dragging the office into the home every evening and weekend is getting you both down? Or is it, as I rather suspect, getting you down but not your husband?

What I imagine is this. There you both are, after a long, hard day fretting about unpaid invoices, the faulty fax machine, the unreliable temp and an unseasonally threadbare order book – and you finally get home.

What you now long for is one or more of the following: dinner out, a good film, a phone call to your daughter and a glass or two of sauvignon blanc. And all he wants to do is bleat about the unpaid invoices, the faulty fax machine, the unreliable temp and the threadbare order book – while expecting a nice hot supper on the table at the same time.

If this strikes a chord, you've got a pig on your hands. My best advice is that you should invent a quite formal routine – and stick to it. Have a proper, expensive, professional sign made reading: THE OFFICE IS NOW CLOSED/OPEN – with one of those little sliding windows. Hang it prominently in your hall at home. When you leave in the morning, ostentatiously flick it from CLOSED to OPEN. On return in the evening, even more ostentatiously, flick it from OPEN to CLOSED.

And always, always get out of your work clothes the moment you get home.

If this doesn't work, change either your husband or your business partner.

Endpiece

Most of us feel that our problems are unique – and we're right. If most problems are people problems, and no two people are identical, it follows that every problem, too, will have its own, distinctive set of fingerprints.

You've probably encountered it yourself: when trying to help a friend in need, you rack your brains for a similar story, preferably with a happy ending. But the friend will have none of it. 'But that was totally different!' they say. And indeed it almost certainly was.

So I have no all-purpose solutions to offer, just some underlying principles or guidelines; not so much solutions as hints on how to approach solutions. There aren't very many and they're very broad.

● You know how you're feeling. Now do your best to imagine what the others are feeling. It's one of the hardest things to do and it requires real effort and imagination; but the rewards can be extraordinary. A lot of problems arise from simple misunderstandings, exaggerated by time. Looking at the same problem through the eyes of others can often have the effect of suddenly getting an optical illusion: the perspective changes, the image clears, the answer presents itself.

● As part of the above, never start a difficult conversation, or send a sensitive letter or e-mail, without trying to put yourself in the place of the recipient. Forget for a moment what you are trying to transmit; think only of how that particular person, in any particular mood, may receive and react. Then reframe and recast as necessary.

● Think things through. If you're a boss, every single difficult decision you make will not only leave at least one person unhappy; it will also establish a precedent. So try to be sure that, in your anxiety to resolve matters, you don't fall for the lure of the temporarily expedient. Consistent inconsistency is a great creator of ever more intransigent problems.

● Practise the challenging art of self-examination. And when you identify error in yourself, concede it freely – and soon. It's evidence not of weakness but of strength. Others will be encouraged to do the same and the lessening of tension will be almost tangible.

● Think about where your responsibilities lie: to your firm, your family, your colleagues, yourself.

Good luck!

JB

READ MORE IN PENGUIN

In every corner of the world, on every subject under the sun, Penguin represents quality and variety – the very best in publishing today.

For complete information about books available from Penguin – including Puffins, Penguin Classics and Arkana – and how to order them, write to us at the appropriate address below. Please note that for copyright reasons the selection of books varies from country to country.

In the United Kingdom: Please write to *Dept. EP, Penguin Books Ltd, Bath Road, Harmondsworth, West Drayton, Middlesex UB7 0DA*

In the United States: Please write to *Consumer Services, Penguin Putnam Inc., 405 Murray Hill Parkway, East Rutherford, New Jersey 07073-2136.* VISA and MasterCard holders call 1-800-631-8571 to order Penguin titles

In Canada: Please write to *Penguin Books Canada Ltd, 10 Alcorn Avenue, Suite 300, Toronto, Ontario M4V 3B2*

In Australia: Please write to *Penguin Books Australia Ltd, 487 Maroondah Highway, Ringwood, Victoria 3134*

In New Zealand: Please write to *Penguin Books (NZ) Ltd, Private Bag 102902, North Shore Mail Centre, Auckland 10*

In India: Please write to *Penguin Books India Pvt Ltd, 11 Community Centre, Panchsheel Park, New Delhi 110017*

In the Netherlands: Please write to *Penguin Books Netherlands bv, Postbus 3507, NL-1001 AH Amsterdam*

In Germany: Please write to *Penguin Books Deutschland GmbH, Metzlerstrasse 26, 60594 Frankfurt am Main*

In Spain: Please write to *Penguin Books S. A., Bravo Murillo 19, 1°B, 28015 Madrid*

In Italy: Please write to *Penguin Italia s.r.l., Via Vittorio Emanuele 45/a, 20094 Corsico, Milano*

In France: Please write to *Penguin France, 12, Rue Prosper Ferradou, 31700 Blagnac*

In Japan: Please write to *Penguin Books Japan Ltd, Iidabashi KM-Bldg, 2-23-9 Koraku, Bunkyo-Ku, Tokyo 112-0004*

In South Africa: Please write to *Penguin Books South Africa (Pty) Ltd, P.O. Box 751093, Gardenview, 2047 Johannesburg*

READ MORE IN PENGUIN

PSYCHOLOGY

How the Mind Works Steven Pinker

This brilliant and controversial book explains what the mind is, how it evolved, and how it allows us to see, think, feel, interact, enjoy the arts and ponder the mysteries of life. 'To have read [the book] is to have consulted a first draft of the structural plan of the human psyche ... a glittering *tour de force*' *Spectator*

The Uses of Enchantment Bruno Bettelheim

'Bruno Bettelheim's tour of fairy stories, with all their psychoanalytic connotations brought out into the open, is a feast of understanding' *New Statesman & Society*. 'Everything that Bettelheim writes about children, particularly about children's involvement in fiction, seems profound and illuminating' *Sunday Times*

Evolution in Mind Henry Plotkin
An Introduction to Evolutionary Psychology

Evolutionary theory holds a vital key to understanding ourselves. In proposing a more revolutionary approach to psychology, Professor Plotkin vividly demonstrates how an evolutionary perspective brings us closer to understanding what it is to be human.

The Care of the Self Michel Foucault
The History of Sexuality Volume 3

Foucault examines the transformation of sexual discourse from the Hellenistic to the Roman world in an enquiry which 'bristles with provocative insights into the tangled liaison of sex and self' *The Times Higher Education Supplement*

READ MORE IN PENGUIN

REFERENCE

Roget's Thesaurus of English Words and Phrases
Edited by Betty Kirkpatrick

This new edition of Roget's classic work, now brought up to date for the nineties, will increase anyone's command of the English language. Fully cross-referenced, it includes synonyms of every kind (formal or colloquial, idiomatic and figurative) for almost 900 headings. It is a must for writers and utterly fascinating for any English speaker.

The Penguin Dictionary of International Relations
Graham Evans and Jeffrey Newnham

International relations have undergone a revolution since the end of the Cold War. This new world disorder is fully reflected in this new Penguin dictionary, which is extensively cross-referenced with a select bibliography to aid further study.

The Penguin Guide to Synonyms and Related Words
S. I. Hayakawa

'More helpful than a thesaurus, more humane than a dictionary, the *Guide to Synonyms and Related Words* maps linguistic boundaries with precision, sensitivity to nuance and, on occasion, dry wit' *The Times Literary Supplement*

Media Law   Geoffrey Robertson QC and Andrew Nichol

Crisp and authoritative surveys explain the up-to-date position on defamation, obscenity, official secrecy, copyright and confidentiality, contempt of court, the protection of privacy and much more.

READ MORE IN PENGUIN

PHILOSOPHY

Brainchildren Daniel C. Dennett

Philosophy of mind has been profoundly affected by this century's scientific advances, and thinking about thinking – how and why the mind works, its very existence – can seem baffling. Here eminent philosopher and cognitive scientist Daniel C. Dennett has provided an eloquent guide through some of the mental and moral mazes.

Language, Truth and Logic A. J. Ayer

The classic text which founded logical positivism and modern British philosophy, *Language, Truth and Logic* swept away the cobwebs and revitalized British philosophy.

The Penguin Dictionary of Philosophy Edited by Thomas Mautner

This dictionary encompasses all aspects of Western philosophy from 600 BC to the present day. With contributions from over a hundred leading philosophers, this dictionary will prove the ideal reference for any student or teacher of philosophy as well as for all those with a general interest in the subject.

Metaphysics as a Guide to Morals Iris Murdoch

'This is philosophy dragged from the cloister, dusted down and made freshly relevant to suffering and egoism, death and religious ecstasy ... and how we feel compassion for others' *Guardian*

READ MORE IN PENGUIN

POLITICS AND SOCIAL SCIENCES

The Unconscious Civilization   John Ralston Saul

In this powerfully argued critique, John Ralston Saul shows how corporatism has become the dominant ideology of our time, cutting across all sectors as well as the political spectrum. The result is an increasingly conformist society in which citizens are reduced to passive bystanders.

Structural Anthropology Volume 1   Claude Lévi-Strauss

'That the complex ensemble of Lévi-Strauss's achievement ... is one of the most original and intellectually exciting of the present age seems undeniable. No one seriously interested in language or literature, in sociology or psychology, can afford to ignore it' George Steiner

The United States of Anger   Gavin Esler

'First-rate ... an even-handed and astute account of the United States today, sure in its judgements and sensitive in its approach' *Scotland on Sunday*. 'In sharply written, often amusing portraits of this dis-connected America far from the capital, Esler probes this state of anger' *The Times*

Values for a Godless Age   Francesca Klug

When the Human Rights Act came into force in October 2000, the United Kingdom at last acquired its own Bill of Rights. In this clear and accessible guide, one of its architects spells out its huge significance for us all. Francesca Klug tells the story of how the idea of rights has evolved from the late eighteenth century to the present day.

READ MORE IN PENGUIN

BUSINESS AND ECONOMICS

Inside Organizations Charles B. Handy

Whatever we do, whatever our profession, organizing is a part of our lives. This book brings together twenty-one ideas which show you how to work with and through other people. There are also questions at the end of each chapter to get you thinking on your own and in a group.

Lloyds Bank Small Business Guide Sara Williams

This long-running guide to making a success of your small business deals with real issues in a practical way. 'As comprehensive an introduction to setting up a business as anyone could need' *Daily Telegraph*

Teach Yourself to Think Edward de Bono

Edward de Bono's masterly book offers a structure that broadens our ability to respond to and cope with a vast range of situations. *Teach Yourself to Think* is software for the brain, turning it into a successful thinking mechanism, and, as such, will prove of immense value to us all.

The Road Ahead Bill Gates

Bill Gates – the man who built Microsoft – takes us back to when he dropped out of Harvard to start his own software company and discusses how we stand on the brink of a new technology revolution that will for ever change and enhance the way we buy, work, learn and communicate with each other.

The Penguin Companion to European Union Timothy Bainbridge

A balanced, comprehensive picture of the institutions, personalities, arguments and political pressures that have shaped Europe since the end of the Second World War.